LONG ROAD OUTTA COMPTON

LONG ROAD
OUTTA COMPTON

Dr. Dre's Mom on
Family, Fame, and Terrible Tragedy

Verna Griffin

 DA CAPO PRESS
A Member of the Perseus Books Group

0474 29577

Designed by Brent Wilcox
Set in 11 point Kepler MM by the Perseus Books Group

Cataloging-in-Publication data for this book is available
from the Library of Congress.

First Da Capo Press edition 2008
First published in the United States in 2005 by Milligan Books
ISBN-13 978-1-56025-987-9

Published by Da Capo Press
A Member of the Perseus Books Group
www.dacapopress.com

Da Capo Press books are available at special discounts for bulk
purchases in the United States by corporations, institutions, and other
organizations. For more information, please contact the Special Markets
Department at the Perseus Books Group, 2300 Chestnut Street, Suite
200, Philadelphia, PA 19103, or call (800) 810-4145, ext. 5000,
or e-mail special.markets@perseusbooks.com.

10 09 08 07 06 05 04 03 02 01

I dedicate this book to my family.
Family Is Gold is our motto.

To all who have had shattered dreams, dashed hopes,
and thwarted plans and have given up somewhere
down the line, I dedicate this book with hopes that it will
encourage you not to give up and to firmly believe that there
is still hope. Never say "can't" because when you do,
you've already set yourself up for failure.

To parents: Don't ever forsake your children. Those same
children may have to take care of *you* someday.

contents

CONTENTS

acknowledgments

My parents, Matthew and Roberta Silverson, for their spiritual guidance and support in every way.

My grandparents, who gave me the opportunity to know them and enjoy them. Without them, there would not have been future generations.

My son Andre Young, for never giving up on his mom through all the hard times and for sharing, caring, and giving support.

My daughter, Shameka Crayon-Miller, for staying close to me and offering her support whenever I needed a hand in every way possible.

My son Tyree Crayon, who is deceased, but his spirit seems to continue to carry me through hard times.

My daughter-in-law, Nicole Young, and my son-in-law, Mark Miller, for adding so much happiness to my children's lives.

My sisters-in-law, Johnnie Young and Elaine Goodman, who remain a part of my family and are always there for me, as well as for their nieces and nephews.

My grandchildren, La Tonya, La Toya, Tyra, Ashley, Cedric, Curtis, Marcel, Tyler, Kion, Summer, Truice, Truly, Andre Jr., King, and Kaylon, for making my life something so grand.

My great-grandchildren, Kani'ya, Amir, and Tatiyana, who made my life even more meaningful to be able to live to see great-grands.

My uncle David and his wife, Aunt Nellie Ruth, who have supported me in everything I've done.

My aunts, Stella, Essie, Sarah, Martha, Ethel, Nellie, and my many cousins who have offered their encouraging words.

All of my friends whom I grew up with and still remain close to today, especially Cheryl Anderson, Bobbie Wilson, Shirley Jackson, Beverly Jackson, Bertie Waters, Ken Craig, Joseph Smith, Andrew Jackson, Nelson Jackson Jr., Darryl Jackson, Tim Jackson, and Lee Jackson.

Special thanks to Mrs. Bobbie Hogue for recognizing the possibility of my life story becoming a book and encouraging me to write.

I would also like to thank Dr. Rosie Milligan, Anita Diggs, and all the other wonderful people who had input in the completion of this book.

Many other relatives and friends, too numerous to mention, but you know who you are.

LONG ROAD OUTTA COMPTON

ONE

Silas and Gracie

IT HAS BEEN SAID that "talent isn't born; it's created." But I believe that there are those rare occasions when talent is born. As I look back over my life, my children's lives, and the lives of the generations before us, it seems to me that the foundation of our successes is rooted in a number of inborn qualities: the determination to do what we set out to do, despite obstacles; a caring and sharing attitude that shows a willingness to do for others; and the courage to make sacrifices and know the importance of a strong family bond. These traits have been passed down in our family for many generations. What other explanation could there be for four generations of gifted individuals in my family?

These traits were first evident in my maternal grandparents, Silas and Gracie Green, seemingly plain and simple black folk who lived in Waskom, Texas. Both Silas and Gracie were born in Greenwood, Louisiana, and came from large families. Silas was one of nine children; Gracie, one of ten. Back in those days, people had long courtships and married young. Since Greenwood was a small town, they probably knew each other growing up and may have been childhood sweethearts. After marrying in 1909, Silas and Gracie moved to Waskom, where all of their eleven children were born.

My grandfather was a striking, strong-willed young man of medium height and dark skin, with a heart of gold. My grandmother was a very fair-skinned lady, who proudly strutted when she walked. They had eleven children: Hettie, Nellie, Silas, Sarah, Ethel, David, Martha, Mary, Lola, Essie, and my mother, Roberta.

Like many black families of their day, my grandparents worked on white people's land in exchange for a place to stay. They were required to give the landowners a portion of the crops that they grew. This was known as sharecropping.

Silas and Gracie were not like most sharecroppers, who typically were poor and barely made a living. They were blessed with a kind and generous landlord who only required that they hand over to him three bales of cotton a year. Beyond that, they were allowed to keep everything that they grew.

Silas and Gracie were hardworking people who produced far more than the three bales per year required by the landlord and were, therefore, able to reap tremendous profits. Aside from growing cotton, they also owned a syrup-producing sugar mill, raised their own farm animals, and grew other crops. Realizing that everyone was not as fortunate as they were, they gladly shared their abundant crops and goods with other sharecroppers. Only after sharing and seeing to it that the family's needs were met did my grandparents sell their excess products.

My grandmother was a talented dressmaker. This proved to be especially beneficial to the family because nine of the eleven children were girls. Gracie would spot a dress at a store in town, buy the fabric, go home, and duplicate the dress exactly. She also made shirts for her husband and the two boys.

My grandfather was what many would call a jack-of-all-trades. He was highly skilled and respected throughout the community. He was a butcher. The meat that he didn't give his family and others, he sold in town. He also helped lay the cross ties for railroad tracks and was skilled at making wagon wheels. He even assisted in preparing bodies for burial. He was also a respected member of the church and assisted the preacher with baptisms.

The landlord's generosity, coupled with a strong work ethic, allowed my grandparents to maintain a better lifestyle than most of the other black families in the small Texas town of Waskom. The Greens lived in a wood-framed, unpainted house, which was quite typical of the family dwellings in the early 1900s. The house had three large bedrooms, a large living room that doubled as a bedroom, a dining room, and a kitchen. A double fireplace heated two of the bedrooms; a wood-burning heater warmed the living room. The family owned a car, a Victrola record player, and a very large collection of 78 records.

The Greens began teaching their children the value of hard work at an early age. All the children had chores. The girls shared the housework, which included washing the dishes, washing and ironing clothes, and milking the cows. The two boys performed outdoor duties, such as chopping wood and feeding livestock.

The children stuck close together. They went to and from school together, played together, and prayed together as faithful members of Union Chapel Baptist Church.

At one point in their lives, my grandparents' faith was clearly tested. Two of their children (Hettie and Mary) fell sick and died. After that, they were prepared to lose their youngest daughter when she came down with a mysterious illness that baffled the doctors, who told them to prepare for Roberta's death. The thought of losing Roberta was devastating to Silas and Gracie.

Bedridden, Roberta couldn't eat or drink and was completely nonresponsive. Then one day, things began to change. Roberta's oldest brother, Silas, went into her room, knelt down by her side, pried her parched lips apart, and forced a teaspoon of water into her slightly open mouth. The water trickled past her lips and slowly went down her throat. Moments later, Roberta began to show signs of life. From that moment on, she began to recover.

To this day, no one really knows what made Roberta sick. Like her mother, Roberta had the gift of sewing and would later become a hardworking seamstress.

Years later, all of Silas and Gracie's children had married and moved away with the exception of Roberta and an older sister, Essie. The four of them stayed in their Texas home until a 1945 chimney fire caused the house to burn to the ground. After searching through the rubble and salvaging what little was left, they moved into a house up the road. Soon thereafter, Essie got married, leaving Roberta as the only remaining child in the household.

In 1949, their eldest daughter, Nellie, suggested that her parents and younger sister move to Los Angeles and stay with her. Nellie and her husband, Julian, had a three-bedroom house. So Silas and Gracie took Roberta and a granddaughter they had started caring for named Regina and moved to Los Angeles.

Lola (whom the whole family called Stella), a free spirit, worked in the garment industry; her husband, Jessie, worked at Ford Motors. After Silas and Gracie had settled in at Nellie's, Stella suggested that Roberta come live with her and her husband and two children in San Pedro, California. Roberta took her sister up on the offer. It was in San Pedro, California, that she met my biological father.

TWO

Roberta, Leslie, Matthew, and Me

SAN PEDRO IS A port city a few miles from Los Angeles. Aunt Stella enjoyed the sea air as well as the hustle and bustle of the diverse and quickly growing town. She, Jessie, and their two children, Lois and Jessie Jr., welcomed Stella's baby sister Roberta into the household, and everyone settled into a family life that was filled with love and laughter.

Uncle Jessie had a friend named Leslie Spratt who hung around the house a lot. What Uncle Jessie and Aunt Stella didn't know until much later was that Leslie was having an affair with Roberta.

My father abandoned my mother as soon as he learned that she was pregnant.

I was born Verna Jean Spratt, on February 4, 1949, in Seaside Memorial Hospital, at Long Beach, California. Leslie insisted that I was not his child.

Mama took me to live with her at Aunt Stella's house. She asked Leslie Spratt to pay her hospital bills. He never did and was never involved in my life. With a screaming six-pound, five-ounce newborn who needed food and many other things, my mother quickly realized that she needed to contribute financially to her sister's household. So she set out to find a job.

Finding work was not an easy task. But finally, after many rejections, my mom found a job at A-1 Kotzin Manufacturing Company, a producer of men's trousers. She labored there as a pieceworker for thirty-three years, making very little money. But she worked hard, seldom missing a day's work. In fact, she would sometimes go to work sick, just so she could earn enough to make ends meet.

My mother was a beautiful woman with a caramel complexion, a slender frame, and a jaunty strut. Her natural pride was evident in the way she walked.

Early one evening after a long, hard day at work, the parking attendant, Matthew Silverson, approached my mom as she walked through the parking lot adjacent to her job. She stopped to hear what Mr. Silverson had to say. He later stated, "I knew I had her when she stopped."

Matthew Silverson was a tall, slender, dark-skinned man who enjoyed making people laugh. He grew up in Little Rock, Arkansas, as one of seven children—five boys and two girls—born to Thomas and Hattie Silverson. Because he felt the need to work to help support his family, his education ended at sixth grade.

They dated for awhile, and then on June 10, 1950, Roberta Green and Matthew Silverson were married. Shortly after their wedding, Matthew Silverson adopted me, and I became Verna Jean Silverson.

We moved into a little place on Newton Street, close to downtown Los Angeles, near the Newton Street Police Station. Our new home was a boardinghouse where many visitors came and went.

Several things about this home and its surrounding neighborhood left an impression on me. For instance, I always looked forward to seeing Mr. Lloyd, the iceman, who delivered ice twice a week. Mr. Lloyd was a robust man who wore an old, worn, heavy cloth jacket, very high wet boots, and a big, black, rubber apron around his neck, which also appeared to be quite heavy. When he appeared in the doorway, he would block the light behind him until he stepped into the house. After he grasped the ice with a pair of giant steel tongs, he would flip it with ease in one smooth motion over his shoulder onto his back. Like a giant uncut diamond glistening in the light, he carried the ice up our stairs into our one-room flat and laid it to rest at the bottom of the icebox. When Mr. Lloyd would leave, my mom always said, "Thank you so much. See you next time." As soon as he got outside, I would hear him yell, "Iceman!" as he continued his rounds.

I was amazed that one block of ice would keep the food in the large metal box cold for three to four days until the iceman came again. My dad had the thankless job of emptying the metal pan under the icebox after it had filled with water that dripped from the melting ice. Since then the icebox has been replaced with a modern convenience called the refrigerator.

Just as intriguing to me as the iceman was seeing the interesting people who frequented the boardinghouse, some of whom were rather friendly. We lived in one room, which served as our bedroom, kitchen, and social place. I could hear just about every noise in the hallway. I had to walk down the hall on the creaky wooden floor to get to the common bathroom shared by all the tenants. I recall seeing the dingy fixtures and smelling old urine seeping into the hallway from the bathroom. The smell may also have come from the floorboards (when tenants didn't make it to the toilet).

When I got the opportunity to get out of the house, I would go through the back gate of the boardinghouse and cross the alley to my aunt Nellie's back gate. I went there often to visit my cousin Lawrence, their younger child. I thought it was great to be able to get to Aunt Nellie's house so easily. Unlike us, Aunt Nellie and Uncle Julian owned their house.

Lawrence had an older sister named Annie who did not live at the house for very long after she moved to California. From what I recall, Annie was busty and hippy. I was a frail child in comparison and often wished I had a figure like hers.

At times, I would stand on the side of Uncle Julian's old car and watch my reflection in the car grow short and wide as I moved back and forth. When I did this, I would imagine myself looking like Annie someday.

THREE

Mrs. Farley

A T ONE POINT, my mom hired a babysitter for me. Her name was Mrs. Farley; she lived around the corner from us, near Fourteenth and Hooper Streets. Mrs. Farley was straight from the "old school." She was very old-fashioned and rigid. A dark-skinned lady of medium height and build, Mrs. Farley was about fifty years of age. She wore a short black wig over her natural hair, which was gray and very nappy.

What I remember most clearly about her was her very ugly habit of dipping snuff. This habit seemed quite out of character for Mrs. Farley, who was otherwise quite a neat person, and always wore a freshly pressed apron. Mrs. Farley's house was immaculate; her insistence on neatness was as rigid as her personality.

On the other hand, Mrs. Farley's husband, who was a slightly overweight, brown-skinned man, was extremely mild-mannered. The Farleys appeared to have very little in common. I didn't see them talking to each other very much. They slept in different rooms: hers was in the front part of the house; his was in the back of the house. They had no children.

In the evenings, Mr. Farley would emerge from his bedroom to eat and watch late-night television. He would often sit on the front porch to water his seemingly perfectly green grass. Mr. Farley spent most of his days at the pool hall at Twelfth and Central. I would often accompany Mrs. Farley downtown to the Grand Central Market to buy groceries and other goodies. On our way, we would sometimes stop by the pool hall. Because it was a warm, friendly place, I could understand why Mr. Farley preferred it to his home.

Although I was not the only child the Farleys kept on a daily basis, I was the only one who stayed there overnight during the week. My dad decided that it was easier to leave me there all week rather than pick me up nightly. I was just two years old when I began staying at the Farleys' house. Everything had been pretty good in my life *until then*.

For some reason, Mrs. Farley treated me differently than the other children. I was the scapegoat for everything that went wrong in the Farley household. I was often blamed and harshly punished for things that I did not do. Many times, I was subjected to Mrs. Farley calling me names such as "little, frail, pigeon-toed girl." She often told me that I was good for nothing and would swat me with a switch from her peach tree.

Most times when Mrs. Farley whipped me, she would grab my dress from the bottom and pull it over my head. Then she whipped me with one hand, while holding the dress together with the other. My arms and hands, as well as my head, were totally enclosed in my dress. I couldn't even attempt to block any of the blows or, for that matter, even see them coming. It was a horrible way to spank a child. I could only cry and scream inside the enclosed chamber of fabric for what seemed to be a lifetime until Mrs. Farley decided my punishment was over.

The only escape I had from this harsh treatment was the Farleys' backyard. It was a very small yard with a well-manicured flower garden, a large peach tree, and an old shed. The backyard stopped where a huge brick wall of a local factory began. The house had a high, wooden back porch. It was so high that I could actually stand under it as a small child. In that backyard, I would daydream of being a dancer, an actress, or someone famous. I dreamed that my mom and dad were so proud of me because of what I had become. Most of all, I dreamed of getting away from Mrs. Farley forever.

As soon as my parents were financially stable, they moved to a one-bedroom back house on Eighty-fifth, near McKinley Avenue.

When I would come home from the Farleys' on weekends, my parents would sometimes allow me to play with the boys who lived in the front house. Those boys really liked to fight. One of them had a bad habit of hitting and spitting on me. When he did that, I would usually wind up running into my house, crying, which brought an end to our playing, at least for the day.

On one occasion, my cousin Lawrence, who was visiting, was standing on the stairs of the apartment building next door. My mom had obviously told him about the trouble I was having with the boys. While I was playing with the three boys, Lawrence decided to issue a warning to prevent any further hitting and spitting. He threatened to throw a big stick down on them if they hit me or spit on me again. They took one look at his hefty size and ran into their house. They would stick their heads out the door from time to time to ask if my cousin was gone yet. After that, they treated me differently, although they still sometimes got the urge to hit me. Mom told me that the next time I was hit, I had better hit back. She had grown tired of me coming home crying and vowed to spank me if it ever happened again. From that day forward, whenever I was hit, I fought back.

My mom and I would walk to my grandparents' house often. They lived on Eighty-seventh Place. My grandmother would fix something special for us to eat. My favorite was hot homemade biscuits with lots of butter and jelly. My grandfather would sometimes take me to the grocery store to buy my favorite foods, such as grapes or raisins.

We spent a lot of time together as a family. My mom and four of her siblings would often get together at my grandparents' house. They would sit around, talking and laughing about the old times. The radio was always set to stations that played New Orleans–style or country music. I remember hearing songs such as "Sixteen Tons" and "Jambalaya."

The family's songs of joy and laughter turned to tears as we were confronted with losing one of our strongest members. I had grown very fond of my grandparents. I was devastated when my grandfather became terminally ill and had to be hospitalized. I can remember how spooky my cousins and I felt on the night we went to visit him. Because he was dying, the hospital allowed us children to visit. As we entered his room, Grandpa was lying in bed with many tubes attached to his body. His breathing was deep, with heavy jolts. The machines that were keeping him alive made rhythmic noises. I don't think Grandpa was even aware that we were in the room. It was very hard to see him, a man whom I had always known as a strong and hardworking person, lying there in that condition, helpless and oblivious to his surroundings. I don't recall anyone saying a word on the way home from the hospital. Everyone's face seemed to say the same thing: we were sad because we knew Grandpa was going to die soon.

The following morning, on April 5, 1954, at 8:45, we got the call that Grandpa had died. As a five-year-old, I had many questions because death was still a mystery to me. After all, I had felt only love from my relatives—my grandparents, my mom, and others. I just could not understand why God would take any of them away from me. My mom, with all her compassion, tried her best to explain it to me, but I was confused and saddened by my grandpa's death. The thought of never being able to see Grandpa again was just so hard for me to accept and understand.

I remember the funeral as if it were yesterday. Before the service began, most of the people who were dressed in black milled around in front of the church. A long, black limousine was parked in front. Inside the church, front and center, was a long, decorated box, which contained my grandpa's body. When the service first began, it seemed like any other Sunday church service—until the part when we all walked toward the open box. As everyone walked around, they seemed to be looking as if they were watching him sleep. When it came my time to look at him, an eerie feeling came over me. To me, the man in the box looked nothing like my grandpa. His face was swollen, his lips wrinkled, and he looked very ashy. I started crying when I realized that my mom was crying. I could not bear to see her cry.

After the service, we all got in the long, black cars and rode for what seemed like forever until we finally came to a big, gated yard that people referred to as the cemetery. It was a place I had never seen before, with lots of statues and monuments. I soon learned that this was the place where my grandpa would be lowered into a deep hole in the ground forever. Losing Grandpa made me so sad, I could barely face the thought of it. But I wanted to be strong for my mom and my grandma. It was really hard to leave my grandpa there in a hole in the ground. At that point in my young life, death did not make any sense to me.

Later that night, my cousin Annie and I slept in the living room on a rollaway bed because our grown relatives took all the other beds. Even with all those people around me, I still had very bad dreams that caused me to sometimes wake up screaming. I realized that I was disturbing everybody in the house, but I couldn't help it. I couldn't get my grandpa's face in that box out of my mind. It was just so frightening.

Days, even weeks, later, I continued to have problems sleeping at night, especially at Mrs. Farley's house, because the room where I slept was always so dark. I would sleep with my head under the covers because I didn't want to see my grandpa's face, which by then, in my mind, had turned into *the monster in the box*.

A few years after my grandfather's death, my parents were blessed to be able to buy their first house, located on 130th Street. I was excited about having a house with a yard that we didn't have to share with anyone else.

Friday was my favorite day of the week because that was when my parents would pick me up from the Farleys.' I'd spend Friday evenings sitting on the Farleys' front porch, anxiously waiting for my parents to pull into the driveway. While I waited, I would count the other cars, wishfully claiming the ones that I hoped to own someday. Just as soon as I spotted my parents' car, I would spring to my feet and run into the house shouting, "My mom is here! My mom is here!" Then I would rush to grab my bag and say good-bye to Mrs. Farley. I moved so fast that I would be ready to jump into the backseat just as soon as the car stopped. Not only did I enjoy being away from Mrs. Farley, but I also liked being with my family on weekends.

First, we would go to the grocery store. All of us took part in choosing items we liked and needed for the upcoming week, including weekend goodies. When we got home, I would run into my bedroom, put my things away, and rejoin my parents in the kitchen to help put away the groceries. In those days, people took their groceries home in boxes, not the bags we use nowadays. After we did that, I enjoyed playing in the boxes. I converted them into many things: cars, skates, and houses. In the end, I would fall into them, tearing them up. My family would end the evening by watching television together.

I felt like I had the most special family, a family who lived in the most special house in the world. Most of the day on Saturday, I spent time enjoying the serenity of my backyard. It was large and filled with peach trees and flowers of all kinds. It was truly a haven for butterflies. I would get up early on Saturday, eat breakfast, and then go straight to the backyard with my butterfly jar in tow. This jar was nothing special. It was any ol' jar I could find. I'd punch holes in the top of it so the butterflies would have air. In a day, I could practically fill my jar with butterflies. They remain one of my favorite creatures on earth. To me, they are the most unique things God ever created. The idea of something as horrendous as a furry worm going into a cocoon and coming out as a beautiful butterfly fascinated me then and still does today. I typically spent the rest of the day playing with the neighborhood kids, something I didn't get to do at Mrs. Farley's house.

But all too soon it would be Sunday—the D-day of my life—the day of the week I dreaded the most. Although it was not the worst day, I knew Sunday meant another week would begin at Mrs. Farley's, and I didn't look forward to it.

The morning would start off fine. We attended Sunday school, where we were taught good lessons. Then we participated in a glorious morning worship at the Providence Baptist Church. Because I was a child, I didn't understand and probably didn't listen to what was being said in the sermon. I did, however, enjoy the choir. Although the choir didn't sing in perfect harmony, they were good enough to get a few hands clapping and feet patting. Every now and then, they would even inspire a few happy souls to jump up and shout. All the excitement that the singing generated kept me awake. It was another story when the preaching started, however. As soon as the sermon began, I'd find myself daydreaming, dozing, squirming, and checking my little Mickey Mouse wristwatch.

Some of the traditions of the church were confusing to me, as they probably were to most children my age. I had more questions than I got answers. For instance, I really didn't understand the offering thing, or *tithes,* as they were frequently referred to in church. In my young mind, I thought, *If we are giving to God by putting our money in the plate, how does the money get to God?* And if people were blessed for giving a small percentage of their income to the church, I wondered if doctors and lawyers, who made a lot of money, received more blessings than poor people on welfare. I worried about whether I would receive any blessings. After all, like most children my age, I had nothing to tithe. Most of the time when I asked such questions, the answers I received left me even more confused. Understand that I was a very curious child who had lots of questions about lots of things. I anxiously waited for the day I would go to school so that I would find some answers to the many questions that plagued me.

I also wondered why pictures of Jesus in the Bible looked different from the Bible's description of the way Jesus was supposed to have looked. I wondered what the Easter bunny had to do with the Resurrection of Christ on Easter Sunday. Did rabbits lay eggs only once a year? Most of all, I wondered what the fat man in the red suit had to do with the birth of Christ. How were the mountains created? How were the stars placed so perfectly in the sky? The universe seemed so amazing and so perfect. Even at that age, I came to the conclusion that a Supreme Being must have created the universe. This early belief in God has remained with me all my life. It has helped me overcome some of the most difficult obstacles and helped me to remain focused on my life's dreams.

In September 1955, the day had finally arrived when I was old enough to attend school. My parents enrolled me in the Twentieth Street School in Los Angeles. I had looked forward to going to school for so long because it would be the beginning of getting answers to all of my questions. To my surprise and disappointment, my first day of kindergarten was terrible.

I was nervous and scared. I cried because I didn't want to stay with all those strangers. The teacher either didn't understand my situation or was just impatient, because she scorned me for my behavior. To make matters worse, the other children in my classroom made fun of me.

They teased me because of the way I looked. I was very pigeon-toed and had to wear corrective shoes. And Mrs. Farley always braided my hair in five little braids because she claimed that would make my hair grow. All the other girls wore cute hairstyles, pretty dresses, and fashionable shoes. I never liked the way Mrs. Farley dressed me. I thought she went out of her way to make me look as unattractive as possible. After complaining to my mom, I finally got a pair of black-and-white saddle oxfords and ribbons to wear in my hair.

Because I was accustomed to playing by myself, it was difficult for me to adjust to playing with others at school. So I continued to play by myself. My cousin Lawrence, who was several grades ahead of me, went to the same school. Though I would see and talk to him on occasion, we didn't get to play together because the playground was separated by grades. Lawrence was three grades ahead of me.

My school life was pretty uneventful until I reached the third grade. There, I finally had a teacher, Ms. Williams, who seemed to take a real interest in me. One day after school, she took me to the local library and got me a library card. From that point on, books became my "best friends." Reading gave me all the things that I had been looking for: words, pride, a sense of accomplishment, self-esteem, and answers to many, many questions. I read all the time. When I wasn't doing chores, I was reading.

Looking back, my experiences at Mrs. Farley's were not all bad. After all, by the age of eight, I had learned to wash my clothes in a ringer-type washer and starch my own dresses by standing on a chair, boiling starch in a big pot. It was a constant challenge to keep the hot starch from burning my hands. I would carry a heavy laundry basket down the steps to the backyard, where I would hang the clothes on a droopy clothesline and hoist it up to the sun with a long board. Of course, I would hope it did not rain, but then again, people say, "It never rains in Southern California." I also learned how to iron my own dresses, make my bed, and clean the kitchen. I really didn't mind doing these chores because I knew that once I finished, I could go back to reading my books. There was, however, one chore that I simply hated to do—emptying the garbage. In those days, trash was burned in an incinerator. So tin cans had to be put in separate containers from the garbage. The "can man" would pick up the cans, and the "garbageman" would pick up the garbage. Separating the trash was no problem. However, the outside garbage bin, which had rats, roaches, and maggots crawling around everywhere, was a horrible sight. Just thinking of it even today still makes my flesh crawl. But, of course, like all adversities, doing these things made me stronger and more prepared for my future role as a homemaker.

Mrs. Farley was a very mean old lady who physically abused me for years. My mom never knew about it until one Tuesday evening when I was in the third grade. Just after school let out for the summer, Mom made one of her regular Tuesday-evening visits. She usually stayed about an hour. We were sitting in the living room, discussing my class work, when I noticed this strange look on her face. She leaned forward slightly and beckoned me to her. I came closer, knowing that she had noticed the large, red, swollen mark on my neck. "Verna, how did that get there?" she asked. I was reluctant to say anything; after all, I had never told my parents about Mrs. Farley's disciplinary tactics. Mrs. Farley had always convinced me I'd done something wrong. I feared that if my mom found out, she would be mad at me, too. Besides, most times, I was so glad to get home to my family on the weekends that whatever abuse I had suffered during the week didn't seem important. Mom broke my silence with a more emphatic, *"Verna, how did that get there?"* Finally, I looked up at her and simply said, "Mrs. Farley." I won't say she "snapped"; she was too much of a lady for that. I'll just say that she confronted Mrs. Farley. I remember Mrs. Farley saying, "I refuse to take care of a kid that I can't whip." During the confrontation, I went out on the front porch because I didn't want to witness what was happening.

It was a quiet night at the Farleys.' In fact, Mrs. Farley barely uttered a word. The next day, she began to help me pack all my belongings and then informed me that I would be going home for good. The next two days were very uneventful; it was as if we were all waiting for Friday to come, when I would leave the Farley household for the last time. When Friday finally arrived, I lay in bed, wondering if I had packed everything because I did not want to have to return for any reason. After bathing and eating a small breakfast, I thought I would get dressed and read until it was time for my parents to come get me.

At about four o'clock, I went to my usual sitting place on the front porch to begin my vigil of waiting and counting the cars for what I hoped would be the last time from the Farleys' porch. I was very quiet, but inside I was overjoyed, knowing that when I left, I would never return. The moment finally arrived when I saw my parents' car round the corner to the Farleys' house for the last time. Although I was glad to be leaving, I also felt a pang of sadness as I waved my final farewell. Life was tough at Mrs. Farley's house, but it was the life that had been familiar to me for those seven years.

FOUR

School Days

FOR ME, THE next day felt like the beginning of a new life. I would wake up every morning, thanking God for removing Mrs. Farley from my life. It was summertime and I could come and go as I pleased, without threat of physical abuse. Lord knows I took full advantage of my newfound freedom.

Dad was wonderful to me. He lacked the ability to read, but could map out directions to get anywhere he wanted to go. He was also excellent at figuring numbers. My father believed that credit was a black man's survival kit; therefore, he paid his bills on time. I don't think my parents were ever late making payments on any of their bills.

My dad would add bills and other necessities on Friday mornings, cash his check Friday evenings, shop for groceries, come home and count out the money for bills and for our savings, get dressed to meet his brothers—and we would not see him again until early Sunday morning.

Aside from my father's weekend habit, he often took his family on outings. Church was our number-one outing, and after church, Dad would treat us to some simple forms of enjoyment. This included visiting family, going to a carnival located on Firestone Street, taking a ride to the city of Wilmington (where we frequented our favorite hamburger stand, called Pop's, located on D Street), or getting an ice cream at Seventy-sixth and San Pedro Streets. Occasionally, we would pack a lunch for an all-day fishing trip down at Cabrillo Beach.

Looking back, I now realize that my mother was a very strong, understanding, and tolerant woman. How she could kiss my father good-bye on Friday night and not see him again until early Sunday morning for years was a mystery to me. When asked where Matthew was, she would simply say, "He's on his mission." I never heard or saw my parents argue or fight, although I would sometimes see my mother saddened by my father's constant weekend excursions. I think she felt that she owed my father a great deal of gratitude. He not only worked a regular daytime job but also worked various evening jobs. He was an excellent provider for his family and had adopted her only child and treated me as if I were his own.

I saw Leslie Spratt once in my life. At the time, I did not know who he was. I was about seven years old and was outside playing at Aunt Stella's house when a man who was visiting Uncle Jessie offered me a dollar. I was reluctant about accepting the dollar. After all, I had been taught all the dos and don'ts about dealing with strangers.

Uncle Jessie assured me that it was okay to take the money. I told the strange man that he had to give Jessie Jr. a dollar too. Uncle Jessie and the strange man both laughed, but he gave my cousin a dollar as well and we hightailed it to the corner store. The only thing that I remember about the man was that he was tall, slender, and brown-skinned. Little did I know, he was my father.

I loved visiting my cousin Lawrence because he told fabulous stories about his experiences in a gang called the Businessmen. They were one of the most notorious gangs in the L.A. area at that time. His gang activity landed him in and out of jail. In fact, he spent much of his life in California's correctional facilities. Nevertheless, he was still one of my favorite childhood cousins. I loved visiting him and hearing about his wild and exciting adventures.

Lawrence had a very large collection of 45 records, which very few people other than me knew about. He was extremely proud and protective of his collection. I was not allowed to touch any of the 45s without his permission. I am not sure what the consequences would have been had I touched them, but I never wanted to find out. If I wanted to hear a record, he would say, "Don't touch it! I will play it for you."

Lawrence was as protective of me as he was of his records. That's why I loved him so much. He made me feel special. At the same time, he could occasionally get rough while we were playing. I had learned to turn negatives into positives. One of the positive things that came out of the abuse I was subjected to during my stay with Mrs. Farley is that my level of pain tolerance is very high.

He liked to use me as a punching bag. At first, it seemed harmless, but one summer day, that rough treatment became serious.

During a discussion, I disagreed with something he said, and then all hell broke loose. He snapped and started hitting me so hard that I wound up on the floor beside the bed in Aunt Nellie's bedroom. Then Lawrence jumped on top of me, put his hands around my throat, and began choking me. I felt like I was going to pass out.

At that point, I reached under the bed and grabbed one of Uncle Julian's steel-toed boots and began swinging it. I managed to clobber him in the forehead. It must have hurt him pretty badly because from that day forward, he never raised his hand to hit me, although he continued to threaten to hurt anyone who wanted to harm me. Despite that incident, I continued to adore him. Unfortunately, I grew up thinking that hitting was a boy's way of showing affection.

When I was home, on a good day, I would leave home as early as eight o'clock in the morning and wouldn't return until the streetlights came on. I spent most of my time playing with the kids next door and across the street. Sometimes I would venture out to other areas in the neighborhood. On other days, it was good just being alone in the serenity of my own backyard. I always felt closer to God when I was outside in nature. I even tried my hand at a vegetable and flower garden. I enjoyed the experience of planting a seed, nurturing it, and watching it grow. I could feel the wind kissing my face, not having any clue as to where it was coming from but knowing that it was the work of God. I saw mountains and other mysterious things and knew that there must be a God.

My neighborhood had an international flavor. It comprised several ethnic groups, including Mexican, black, Japanese, white, and Hawaiian families. All of the groups seemed to blend well together.

I had friends from each of the diverse cultures, many of whom remain in my life today. I believe my early childhood experience of living in a culturally mixed neighborhood gave me the ability to mix well in any group. I learned to get along with everyone and to respect others for who they were from the inside out. Life was good.

Although my mom allowed me the freedom to roam when she was home, on the weekends, when she was working, it was a different matter. Because she did not want me to be left alone, she found another lady to babysit me. This babysitter, Ms. Leona, lived across the street.

Ms. Leona also babysat another little girl, named Trudy. Trudy and I had quite a lot in common. We were the same age, both only children, and we liked a lot of the same things. Even though we were in the same grade, Trudy was a little more scholastically advanced than I was. This turned out to be a plus. Now that I had been introduced to reading, I felt that I could conquer anything. It was fun yet challenging to compete with Trudy every day. Our time together was short-lived, however, because she suddenly stopped coming to Ms. Leona's house. I wasn't sure why. All I knew was that I missed her.

It was fun at Ms. Leona's house until Trudy stopped coming. Ms. Leona would frequently have adult company. There was never anyone for me to play with anymore. I found myself bored and very lonely.

One day I skipped to the store, trying to remember what Ms. Leona had told me to pick up. As I reached what was considered the worst house on the block, I suddenly became ill and passed out. An older couple who seemed to live like hermits were in the old, run-down house. The couple dressed in very old clothes and never talked to anybody. Their windows were covered with cardboard. I had heard that they used kerosene lamps for lighting because they had no electricity. I could see puffs of smoke billowing out through a vent at the top of the house from the wood-burning stove. To this day, I have no idea why I passed out in their yard. Someone in the house saw me lying on the ground and came out to see if I was all right. I could hear their voices, although they sounded very distant.

When I came to, a lady from the house was wiping my face with something wet, and I could see a man who I thought was her husband going to get Ms. Leona. This was the first time anyone had known them to speak to others in the neighborhood. From that day forward, the little old couple always waved and greeted me every time I passed by. Eventually, they were forced to move because the authorities condemned their house.

When Ms. Leona moved, I was overjoyed. It seemed to me that when babysitters quit, there was an opportunity for me to spend more time with my mother. I often dreamed of the day when she would no longer have to go to work, so then she could stay home with me all the time. Well, after Ms. Leona left, I got the next best thing to my mother. My grandma Gracie Green came to stay with us. I never had to go to a babysitter again.

Just as I had become familiar with the neighborhood and its surroundings, the summer ended. It was time for me to enter the fourth grade. That morning, my mother took me to the office of Mark Twain Elementary School, where I was assigned to a classroom. I remember feeling lonely and scared when my mother said good-bye because I was among strangers. The adjustment to being alone in a new school, meeting new students, and experiencing new teachers nearly sent me into a state of hysteria. Fortunately, the lady who escorted me to my new classroom was very nice. I was comforted by her friendliness and felt a little less nervous as I approached the classroom. When I entered it, I was surprised that the teacher and the students greeted me with friendly faces. After introducing me to the class, my new teacher, Ms. Gilliam, showed me to my desk. For the first time, I began to feel at ease. I felt that I could leave my past behind and create a new life in this improved environment.

The class was made up of fourth and fifth graders. As a fourth grader, I took full advantage of learning from the more advanced fifth graders. This class was the stepping-stone for my transformation from a timid girl to one who believed that the sky was the limit. I became a straight-A student. My parents were so proud of me that they took every opportunity to show off my report cards to our family and friends.

I became a sponge for knowledge. On some occasions when I went to the store with my parents, I would ask for a book instead of a toy. I spent more and more time in the library. I read everything, and I could spell anything. I became one of the top students and finally acquired the gift of self-esteem.

The summer between fourth and fifth grades was much like the previous summer. I spent most of my time becoming more familiar with my neighborhood and new friends from school.

I entered fifth grade with a ready-set-go attitude. I felt as though I could conquer anything. I eagerly tackled my studies. Once again, I became one of the top students in my class. My favorite subject was mathematics. I became an excellent speller, competing and winning spelling bees. I also developed award-winning penmanship.

One day, a classmate's mother came to school to see a teacher. When I saw her, I was shocked by her appearance. This parent was dressed very shabbily and wore shoes that had the backs worn down. Her feet were dry and crusty, and she wore rollers in her hair that appeared to have been in for days. The dress she wore looked like a muumuu and had grease spots and other residue splattered on the front. When the mother left, all the kids in the class laughed, including me. We teased and laughed at the boy, too. His feelings were quite hurt. In fact, he started to cry. I immediately felt great compassion for him and insisted that everyone stop laughing and ridiculing him.

I vowed never to show up, representing my family, without looking my very best. Looking your best was something that my mom had always drilled into my head, anyway. "Never leave home without looking decent; you never know whom you might meet," she would say. My mother said quite a few other things that I usually didn't remember until I was in a situation where I needed her wisdom. Mom did repeat the following pearls of wisdom that still remain with me today: "There is no such thing as 'can't.'" "If at first you don't succeed, try, try again." "If you don't accomplish your goal one way, turn around and approach it from a different angle." And last, "If you don't want to deal with the devil, stay off of his grounds."

At the end of each school year, we would receive a final report card, which would include the name of our teacher for the upcoming year. I had heard terrible things about one particular sixth-grade teacher, Mr. Wright. Everybody dreaded the thought of going to his class. When we received our report cards, everyone opened them with the seriousness that one would search a ballot for their favorite candidate. Throughout the class, you could hear expressions of excitement and dismay. I carefully opened mine with a sense of great anticipation, only to find that I had the teacher who had been described as a demon.

The summer after fifth grade was basically like all my other summers had been, except that Ms. Leona moved away and the Broom family moved into her old house. My mother liked them because they seemed to be a very religious and well-rounded family. There were three boys and three girls, all of whom seemed to be no more than a year apart. The Brooms' home became my home away from home. In fact, I was there all day, every day, until my parents got home.

As the summer drew to an end, it was time for back-to-school shopping. This time, we chose clothes that were more grown-up. My mom made a valiant effort to purchase everything I wanted to encourage me to do my best in school. I spent the night before the start of sixth grade organizing my outfits and planning the order in which I would wear them.

On the first day of school, I woke up early because I was excited. I got up in time to have breakfast with my parents before they left for work. I made sure that my clothes looked right and that my hair was styled to perfection. As I took one last look in the mirror and gave myself a final approval, I grabbed my school supplies and headed across the street to walk to school with the Broom clan.

The first day in Mr. Wright's class was very different from my previous classroom experiences. Mr. Wright attempted to develop his students' abilities by making threats. If he believed a student had academic ability, he would push that student to the limit. Even though he was labeled as the meanest teacher at Mark Twain, he definitely made a positive impact on my life.

In those days, corporal punishment was still allowed in schools. Mr. Wright always kept a paddle on his desk. If students answered questions incorrectly when called upon, he would swat them. I did everything I could to avoid being called on, but Mr. Wright seemed to love calling on me. For some reason, he thought I knew the answers to all of his questions. It was not that I didn't know most of the answers; I just didn't want to risk getting swatted if I happened not to know the answer. Occasionally, I would give the wrong answer, and he would say, "Silverson, come here." He would demand that I hold out my hand and then would give me a rap across it. Those swats left me feeling as if part of my hand had come off on the paddle. Because I would take the punishment without crying, he referred to me as a "tough cookie." After the swat, I couldn't wait to return to my seat so that I could place my hand against the desk. The cold metal seemed to offer me some quick relief.

That year, Mark Twain Elementary School developed its first athletic program. Mr. Wright thought I was smart enough and tough enough to be captain for our volleyball, baseball, and track teams. I led all three teams to undefeated seasons. By the end of the year, I was amazed by my own accomplishments. The students and teachers knew me as both academically and athletically strong, and I was very popular. Mr. Wright's belief in my abilities inspired me to continue to do well.

When the year ended, I was ready to graduate from Mark Twain. We spent time practicing the march, the speeches, and the songs. My mom took me shopping for the prettiest outfit. It was a most exciting time indeed. The thought of going on to junior high left me feeling as if I was beginning a new and exciting life.

Graduation day was wonderful. My mom sat proudly in the audience as I walked across the stage to receive my diploma. I said good-bye to classmates, some whom I would never see again. Several others went on to Vanguard Junior High School with me.

I had another good summer (as all of my summers had been since I stopped going to Mrs. Farley's). I added new blocks to my normal neighborhood play territory and added new kids to my list of "hang-out buddies." I even found a neighborhood that I didn't know existed just west of San Pedro Street. For years, I would pass by an area that consisted of a large field full of weeds and an old abandoned two-story house at the far end. During my last year in elementary school, there was quite a bit of construction going on in my neighborhood, much of it on the abandoned lot. The new junior high school that I would be attending was built there, as well as a new department store.

As the land was cleared for the department store, I discovered another community behind it. This community, though new to me, was actually not new at all. In fact, it was an old community that carried the nickname Plumnelly.

Why Plumnelly? As legend has it, it was called that because it was said to be "plum out of the city" and nearly "out of the world." Sounds corny, but that's what we named it as children.

I met lots of new and wonderful people in my new territory. In fact, many of them remain my friends today. Strangely enough, as close as Plumnelly was to my old stomping grounds, it was quite different from the neighborhoods to which I had grown accustomed. Oil fields were there, as well as a dairy, horse stables, farm animals in backyards, and many open fields. I thought this was about as close to country living as I would ever get.

Many of the kids from Plumnelly were about my age, although there were quite a few older and younger kids, too. Our neighborhood was divided into three groups. The oldest group was called the "Beat Boys." The group in my age bracket was called "Plumnelly." And the youngest group was referred to as the "Alley Tramps." We were not gangs. We all got along well and looked out for one another.

As I thought about going back to school at the end of the summer, I realized that going from elementary school to junior high school meant not only changing schools but changing systems as well. I would now have to get used to having several teachers during the day, as opposed to one teacher all day. I would also have to become accustomed to new classmates. I looked forward to these and other new life challenges as I approached my teenage years.

Then it was time for junior high school.

Vanguard Junior High School was brand-new and right around the corner from where I lived. The first day of the seventh grade was exciting. Everything was new: the school, books, and chairs. What I remember most about that day is that I met Bertie, another nervous new seventh grader, who would become my lifelong friend.

Bertie was very outgoing, friendly, and bright. She was an attractive girl with humongous lips and large brown eyes. We found comfort in each other. It turned out that we had most of the same classes together. And Bertie lived in my favorite new play terri-tory—Plumnelly. We began doing many things together: playing, singing, studying, and competing for the best grades.

My elective class was home economics. That included sewing. All those countless hours of sitting next to Grandma, learning to sew, really paid off in that class.

Grandma was unquestionably one of the best grandmothers in the world. She would sit in her rocking chair making quilts, while I sat close by, catching all the pieces that she discarded. I used the scraps to make doll clothes. I would sit beside her wide-eyed, lis-tening to her stories about our family history. By sitting at her side, I not only was entertained and educated by her stories but also learned to sew quite well. On one occasion, I made a skirt for my-self completely by hand. When I wore that skirt to school the next day, I received lots of compliments. I responded proudly, "I made it." My grandma was willing to give what she had to me. I really learned a lot from her and from her storytelling.

When it came to fashion, my grandma was a woman before her time. She inspired the fashion sense of her children, grandchil-dren, and great-grandchildren. Because of her teaching, I had a head start on everyone in my class. I even began to feel that sewing and fashion design were my true talents. I received an A-plus on my first project, which was a lady's three-piece suit. In fact, my project was showcased in the school's fashion show. As usual, my mom sat proudly in the audience while my fashions were dis-played. Having her there at school events made me feel really good and boosted my overall morale. She even surprised me with my first sewing machine soon after the fashion show.

I tried very hard to stay focused and motivated about my new-found love for fashion, as well as my academic studies. I managed to remain on point throughout the seventh grade.

The eighth grade was a totally different story, however. By then, most everyone in my grade knew me for one reason or another. I was gaining popularity by being a clown. My mom was called in for conferences at my school, and afterward she would have long, serious talks with me. I hated to see my mother down, so I would try to do better. It seemed that I was caught in a web of confusion. Part of me wanted to do well, and the other part craved the negative attention.

I started getting thrills out of figuring out ways to get myself in trouble. I did stupid stuff like putting a tack on the teacher's seat or rubbing color chalk on paper towels and rubbing it on someone's face. I was constantly being sent to the principal's office.

I completely lost focus, and by midyear, I was expelled for the rest of the school year and sent to Willowbrook Junior High School. This school was used as a punishment to get me away from the group that I was hanging out with.

This was the same year that my mother told me that Matthew Silverson was not my father. I think my mom waited until she felt I was old enough to understand. It didn't work. I was rebellious. For a short time, I didn't want Matthew to say anything to me and didn't want to be in the same room with him. It was as if I blamed him for the situation. I was angry with Matthew, who loved me enough to go to court to adopt me, instead of hating Leslie Spratt, who, in that same court, denied that he was my father. By then the mental picture that I had of the man who gave me a dollar had long faded.

It only took me a few weeks to regroup, though, and then Matthew and I were fine again. I didn't ask about Leslie Spratt again until I decided to write my life story. It was only then that I learned that he had died. I don't know how or when.

I only got into one actual fight in school. The fact that I did not back down (and in some people's eyes, I actually won the fight) gave me the reputation of being a bad girl. This tended to keep negative encounters down to a precious few. It was kind of nice not having to worry about fighting or defending myself because I could just concentrate on getting good grades.

Being respected for my intelligence and my wit was a really cool thing. No one seemed able to surpass me in these two areas. In fact, my intelligence turned out to be my best asset. This was the good side of me, but the bad side continued to surface.

Going to Willowbrook was a lesson I would never forget. The school was located several blocks from my house at the corner of El Segundo Boulevard and Willowbrook Street. I rode to school with a neighbor who attended Centennial High School, which was near Willowbrook. Even though I made new friends there, I felt lost without my friends from the neighborhood. I especially missed Bertie, who remained at my old school. After school, I couldn't wait to get home to visit with her and other friends in Plumnelly.

Once I was transferred to Willowbrook Junior High School, I took advantage of trying harder to start over. I didn't know anybody when I first got there, so that helped a little. I was anxious to be good so that I would return to Vanguard the next school term, as promised by the principal.

It wasn't hard for me to meet people, and I seemed to be a magnet for those who liked to stay in trouble. I ended up with a group that enjoyed ditching school. I didn't like Willowbrook, so ditching school was all right by me. The new friends and I would catch a bus and go hang out in an area called Huntington Park at a shopping center. A couple of times, hanging out with them brought me back to reality, and I didn't want to ditch school anymore. By the time the school term was coming to a close, I was ready to get serious about school and vowed that the clowning must stop. Needless to say, my grades had suffered, and I barely made it through the eighth grade. I did make it, though.

When eighth grade was over and the long-awaited summer of '63 finally arrived, Plumnelly was my playground. Boy, did we have fun playing baseball and all sorts of other games! We loved hanging out, making fun out of anything and everything. Neighborhood family parties went on throughout the summer. The parties were packed with kids from all over our neighborhood. Music was in the air. We all thought we were musically inclined. On occasion, we would break out with jam sessions in the small garage at the Jacksons' house, my favorite family of friends. The sound of music, piano, drums, as well as alto and tenor saxophones could be heard throughout the neighborhood.

FiVE

Theodore

SOME OF US who really thought we could sing formed a singing group called the Four Aces. We practiced at my house every chance we got. The Four Aces wrote lyrics and played piano. Our voices blended beautifully in harmony. In order for the guys in the neighborhood not to be outdone, they formed their own little singing group, called the Romells.

One member of that group was Theodore Young. When summer was over, we still got together in the evenings and on weekends, mostly studying or just hanging out. Theodore went to Centennial High School.

Theodore was a tall, dark-skinned, outgoing boy who displayed leadership qualities. All of the guys in the neighborhood liked hanging around him. I was in seventh heaven when he asked me to go with him. He chose me out of all the girls in the neighborhood, and I felt special. Theodore and I started getting closer and closer day by day.

He would sometimes come and knock on my window at night, and I would sneak out to be with him. At this young time of my life I truly thought that this was love.

When I started the ninth grade back at Vanguard Junior High School, I had an altogether new attitude about learning and vowed to stay out of trouble and never to be kicked out of school again. I began aggressively working toward improving my grades to the level that they were before.

The school year passed pretty quickly. On graduation day, I was thankful for the opportunity to receive my diploma. There had been days when I thought it would never happen. After graduation, I looked forward to another fun-filled summer.

But it wasn't too long before Theodore and I found ourselves falling asleep a lot in the middle of the day, and I started getting sick. A few times my mother walked in from work and found both of us sitting in the large chair asleep. I think that this drew her suspicions. When I told her that everything was fine, she stared at me for a long moment and then said, "I'm too old of a cat to be fooled by a kitten."

My mother decided that I should go to the doctor. The first time at the doctor's office, I felt afraid and ashamed. I was so small, the doctor couldn't tell whether I was pregnant, so he asked us to come back in one month. This was a relief because it meant there was still a small chance that I was not pregnant. I wanted a miracle to happen.

I had heard of morning sickness, but I was sick morning, afternoon, and evening. The symptoms continued the entire month.

The next doctor's appointment came around really fast. By that time, I had convinced myself to be okay with whatever the findings were. After all, there was nothing that I could do if I were pregnant. The test came back positive.

Theodore didn't seem surprised. I think he was more prepared for the news than I was. My mother and father had a talk with us and suggested we do what they thought was the right thing: get married. I loved Theodore, so the idea of being with him all the time seemed wonderful to me. After meeting with Theodore's mother, I was not sure about the marriage thing anymore. She was totally against it. My mom was adamant about us getting married.

From that point, my life changed forever. I was no longer the young schoolgirl getting in trouble for ditching class or the young lady concentrating on her studies. I was suddenly a woman, forced into making grown-up decisions long before I was ready. Many of the decisions I made at that point left me very confused. Because our carelessness resulted in pregnancy, Theodore and I were forced to make decisions that changed our lives in drastic ways.

Theodore was seventeen; I was only fifteen. We knew what we had done was wrong and were willing to do whatever it took to make amends.

So, on August 22, 1964, Theodore and I were married in his mother's living room with a small group of our friends as witnesses. I became Verna Jean Young.

SIX

Married Life

BECAUSE THEODORE AND I were both unemployed, we moved in with my parents. He did not have much luck looking for employment. In 1964, an unskilled, inexperienced seventeen-year-old stood little chance of finding work. Unlike today when young people can find jobs at places such as fast food restaurants, movie theaters, and coffee shops, those types of jobs were not plentiful back then.

Theodore wanted to be a good husband. After returning from a job search, he would come home sad and disappointed. Mom, Dad, and I would offer words of encouragement.

One of the neighborhood mothers encouraged me to apply for welfare, so I did. Unlike today's welfare system where applicants go to the welfare office, social workers, or "workers," as they were called at that time, visited the homes of all welfare applicants. They inspected the homes like Nazi storm troopers to determine if an applicant was in dire-enough need of "relief," or welfare.

They did not want to see even the simplest items of convenience in your home, such as toasters, televisions, mixers, and radios. Even jewelry, no matter the worth, had to be carefully hidden from the intrusive eye of the worker to prevent the applicant from being disqualified.

On the day of my appointment, my worker showed up, ready to tear me down. She was armed with a questionnaire that asked for very personal information. Some of the questions were so embarrassing that I refused to answer them. As a result, my welfare application was denied.

My dad started to get antsy because our future plans were not developing fast enough. He became upset with the situation and started to express his disappointment. We did not want to cause problems between my mom and dad, so when neighbors offered us a room in their home, we took it.

Mr. Willis, a neighborhood construction worker, convinced the owner of the construction company to hire my new husband. We did not have a car, so Mr. Willis was also kind enough to pick up Theodore for work each day. The job was tenuous, because construction is a good-weather occupation. During the first three months, it seemed to rain constantly. And when it rained, Theodore didn't work. I eventually started to feel guilty about having Theodore go through so much. When he did work, however, he contributed to the household and even managed to save a little money toward getting our own place.

During my pregnancy, I walked, read, and shopped a lot. I collected Blue Chip stamps and spent many hours selecting items that I could buy for my baby's layette. I was also a frequent visitor to a shop in Compton, called Hilda's Children's Shop. Hilda's had the most unique items that you could ever find for infants and children. I would carefully put together new outfits that I had purchased. As I shopped, I would often recount in my mind the mean things people said about me, like, *Look at her. She's going to be a baby taking care of a baby. She's just a little fast thing who's going nowhere.* Or, *She ain't going to be nothing, and her baby ain't either.* Hearing these things obviously made me angry, but they also strengthened my resolve that I was going to take good care of my baby.

When I got close to my due date, a pain like I'd never felt before sent everybody jumping and running to get me to L.A. County General Hospital, where my first child would be born. After I was admitted and prepped, I was taken to the labor room to await the wonderful moment. Meanwhile, absolutely no one could help me get through the pain I was feeling during labor. I just lay there, constantly preparing for the next pain to hit. The doctor checked on me occasionally to see how close I was to delivering. When I got to the point where I really just couldn't take the pain any longer, it seemed that the doctor appeared out of nowhere to give me the epidural.

Shortly after that, the most wonderful thing that could ever happen to a woman happened to me. Even though he seemed reluctant to come into this world, at 10:56 A.M., February 18, 1965, my son Andre Romell Young was born. He was a screaming little bald-headed, seven-pound bundle of joy. We chose Romell as his middle name after Theodore's singing group.

When the baby and I were released from the hospital, we went back to live with my parents for a few more months. Having a new baby meant a whole new way of living. Our days and nights included feedings, diaper changes, and formula preparations. Andre became my main concern. I thoroughly enjoyed being a mother. I read many books on baby care so that I would be fully equipped to be the best mother I could possibly be.

In June 1965, just four months after Andre was born, the Watts Riots broke out. This incident changed the world's perception of race relations in America and actual rioting in the streets was broadcasted on television. Those riots are believed by many historians to be the worst civil unrest in America since the Boston Tea Party or the labor riots of 1908.

I had never witnessed anything like it in my lifetime. I saw buildings burning, innocent people being beaten, looting taking place, and complete destruction of property. It was really scary. Seeing National Guard tanks rolling through the neighborhood with armed military guards enforcing a ten o'clock curfew was astonishing.

Most people look back on this historic event and find that several good things came about as a result. For instance, black people in Los Angeles came together and worked with the authorities to prevent such violence in the future. They even parlayed the situation into opportunities for black people.

After the event was behind us, Theodore and I continued to search for a decent place to live and gainful, steady employment.

No one wanted to rent to such a young couple. Luckily, Theodore's stepfather, Richard, owned a house that he occasionally used as his "getaway" on 135th Street. The house had two bedrooms and was completely furnished. He recognized the fact that we were having a hard time finding a place and was nice enough to let us rent the home for only eighteen dollars per week, not including utilities.

Shortly after this, Theodore was able to land a job at a company that did laundry for restaurants and hospitals. It seemed that things had turned around and were finally going our way. We started to feel like a real family.

Andre was a very friendly baby who would go to anyone. His four young uncles and two aunts, and what seemed like the entire neighborhood, loved to take turns holding him. When he was a few weeks old, like all parents, we were plagued with sleepless nights and early morning wake-ups. At first, we thought Andre cried only when he was hungry. Later, we found out that he was crying mostly because he wanted noise and people around him. *He didn't like the quiet.*

Andre loved hearing music, even as an infant. It seems that he was born with a love for music. When I look back on his life, I think he began to develop this love when he was only a few months old. That was when I first noticed the soothing effect that music had on him. When music was playing, he would lie content and look around as if he were searching for the direction from which the sound was coming. As long as he was full and dry, he would lie there listening to the music until he fell asleep.

Andre also loved to eat. So much so that doctors recommended that we begin giving him baby food early. We initially fed him applesauce and rice cereal. He grew fast and became a big baby in a very short time. In the neighborhood, people teased me on a daily basis about Andre's size. "That boy is almost as big as you," they would say. Or, "You're going to need a wheelbarrow to carry that boy soon."

My grandmother felt Andre was far too heavy for a little person like me to tote around. She also realized that I didn't have much choice because our money was tight. One day she surprised us with a brand-new stroller. Theodore had been raised with an old-fashioned attitude that women were not supposed to work outside of the home. I spent my days cleaning, cooking, reading, and caring for our child. I carried out my job as a housewife and mother meticulously.

By the time Andre reached nine months old, he was potty-trained and walking. I was amazed when he started pulling himself up on the furniture and was even more astounded when he let go and began walking. He never bothered to crawl. Andre seemed to do most things at an earlier age than normal. It seemed he learned to speak very clearly from the time he said his first words. People couldn't believe it when I told them how young he was.

I should have known that Andre would be gifted with words. I can remember my mother teaching him poetry when he was a young child. She loved poetry and taught it to him when he was three years old. Of course, hip-hop was not even thought of back then, but I suppose God knew that Andre would be instrumental in creating an art form that combined his gift with words and his love for music.

One night while Andre and I were at home alone, I heard the side gate scraping against the house, as if it were being opened. Frightened, I stopped dead in my tracks and listened closely. I then heard footsteps coming up the walkway leading to the back steps. A man's silhouette appeared through the shade-covered window as the light from the kitchen reflected on it.

I slowly eased off the sofa, walked across the room, carefully putting one foot in front of the other, creeping so as not to make a sound. When I finally got to Andre's room, I slowly picked him up and went into the hallway to call my mother. I then went to my room, walking backward all the way to make sure that the prowler would not surprise me.

Once back in my bedroom, I calmly waited for my mother or the police to come. I hadn't heard any glass break or the door creak, so I knew the prowler had not yet come into the house. Andre, who was asleep when I picked him up, did not awaken the whole time, even though I was squeezing him intensely. Time seemed to go by slowly. I fearfully waited, wishing that someone would come soon. I could hear the person testing the back door-knob, turning it back and forth, to see if it was unlocked. My heart was racing, but I didn't know what would happen if I tried to escape. All of a sudden, I heard the sound of a car door close, then another right after it. *Two people . . .* , I thought. *Must be my mom and dad.*

I rushed to the door, opened it, and to my relief, there stood my parents. I told them everything that had happened in what seemed like one single breath. My dad went to the back door and grabbed the doorknob, expecting to pull the door open. Instead, the doorknob came off in his hand. My heart sank because I knew it was not my imagination. The loose doorknob was a clear indication that I had almost become a crime statistic.

After Dad replaced the screws in the doorknob, my parents prepared to leave, assuring me that everything was going to be all right. I did not want them to go, at least not until Theodore got home. But they had to get up early for work in the morning. After checking around the house, Dad felt that the danger was over. Besides, Theodore was due home very shortly.

Just as soon as they left, the mystery person returned. I could hear the footsteps again, approaching the back gate. Just then, I heard Theodore and his friends approaching the front door. I ran to him with Andre in my arms and frantically told him the story. They looked around, but didn't see a soul. Everyone left the kitchen except me. I calmed down and began preparing some of their favorite snacks. Suddenly, I heard the noise again! I ran out of the kitchen to alert Theodore that the intruder was still around.

He and his friends went to the back door, into the backyard, and jokingly called out, "Here, kitty, kitty." Then Theodore immediately ran to the front door and threw it open. He chased the would-be intruder down the sidewalk, but was unable to catch him.

After that terrible experience, he hired one of his friends to come over every evening, armed with a shotgun, to guard Andre and me while he was at work.

While my husband was very protective of me, he was also high-strung, jealous, and, to my mind, abusive. If I went to the neighborhood store and stayed too long, he would get physical with me. If I engaged in what he considered a prolonged conver-

SILAS GREEN   GRACIE LEE GREEN

Verna's grandparents.

Upper window: Hettie Green-Young. Top row: Essie Green, Lola Green, Roberta Green (Verna's mother). Bottom row: Hettie's children, Saberia, Daniel, and Gracie Young.

Providence Baptist Church usher board. Verna's father is top right, and her mother is bottom right. Verna's mother joined the church in 1950 after marrying Verna's father, who had been there for several years.

Verna's parents, Matthew and Roberta Silverson.

Verna's fifth birthday party. She is the little girl in the white dress with the bow in her hair, and her cousin Lawrence is in the white shirt. The others are neighborhood children.

Verna and Theodore on their wedding day, August 22, 1964.

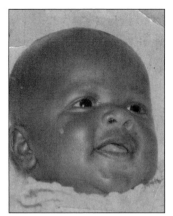

Andre, three months old

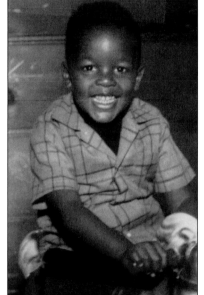

Andre Young,
age three.

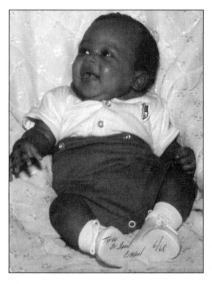

Tyree DuSean Crayon,
three months old.

Andre, age seven.

Curtis and Verna Crayon
on their wedding day.

Andre (age eight) and
Tyree (age five).

Shameka Denee Crayon,
seven months old.

Andre with Shameka,
congratulating Tyree on
his graduation from
elementary school.

Andre, tenth grade.

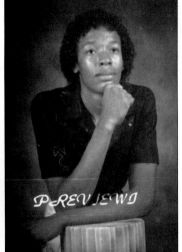

Andre, senior year, 1983.

Andre on prom night.

Andre, age nineteen, with his first child, La Tonya Young.

Tyree Crayon and Warren Griffin III (Warren G).

Tyree's high school graduation day, June 1986.

Tyree modeling in
Verna's modeling group.

Tyree and son, Cedric.

Cedric at two years, seven
months, seventeen days,
April 20, 1990.

sation with any of his male companions, he would get physical with me.

At that time, the only way I saw to stop this was to simply stay in my room until everyone left. I spent so much time out of sight when Theodore's friends were around, some of them probably didn't even know that he had a wife. Looking back, I think that Theodore's hostility came from frustration. He saw himself as a failure.

Theodore never got physical with me while we were dating, so it came as a shock to me. I always felt guilty about it. After all, I had forced a boy to grow up and be a man in less than nine months.

At one point, Theodore lost his job. I am not sure if it was due to tardiness or what. I never found out the reason. All I know is that after he lost the job at the laundry, he began selling drugs to make ends meet. With drugs came a lot of unknown people. We constantly had to watch for the police and became very distrustful of strangers.

At first, people would buy their drugs and leave. But it got to the point that they would stay and use the drugs in our house. This was not something that I wanted Andre subjected to. When I saw a constant flow of strangers around the house, I wondered who they were. More than that, I wondered what had happened to my dream of a happy home. Sometimes I could look right outside my bedroom window and see suspicious-looking cars parked down the street. I feared that we would one day get busted. Deep down, I feared going to jail and having my baby taken away from me.

It's been so long since Theodore and I were together that I don't remember any of his distinctive traits with the exception of his violent temper. At first, Theodore wasn't using drugs—just selling them. But our financial struggles continued, and I think he ended up using drugs to gain some temporary relief from his problems. I didn't indulge in drugs. I was too busy watching out the window for strange cars and newcomers and taking care of my son.

The stale odor of marijuana was so strong that not even daily cleaning could get rid of it. It was embedded in the furniture, drapes, bedding, and the walls—everywhere. Our house was not a happy home anymore and had not been for some time. I really did not know what to do about it.

Sometimes, I would lay in bed at night, thinking back to my experiences at Mrs. Farley's. I realized I had ended up in another bad situation in my life, but this time, it was my own fault.

One day, I decided I just couldn't take it anymore. After another physical incident with Theodore, I packed up all of Andre's and my things, left that 135th Street house, and went back to stay with my parents. I wasn't concerned about Theodore coming after me because my dad did not play around, and Theodore knew it.

After moving back in with my folks, I tried to get my life together. I ran across an advertisement announcing the Neighborhood Youth Corp. (NYC). It was one of the many government social programs that emerged after the Watts Riots. NYC was created for youths, ages sixteen to twenty-one, who had either dropped out of school or were simply having a hard time finding jobs. Young people under twenty-one years old needed their parents' written consent in order to work. Because I was married and underage, I needed my husband's, rather than my parents', consent. There was no way in hell that I would risk getting Theodore's consent. *I didn't need anything from him anymore,* I thought. Therefore, I decided to forge his signature. This was my first act in asserting my independence, and it felt good.

My first position was as an office clerk, working side by side with my supervisor, Norida Comminey, who was known in the office as Chickee. Chickee and I got along quite well and developed a pretty close relationship. I was her "right hand" at work and a friend away from the workplace.

Theodore's mother agreed to watch Andre while I was at work. During this time, Theodore tried to get me to come back to him. In a matter of weeks, he sweet-talked me into coming back home, with promises never to be physical with me again. I went back to 135th Street to live with him, hoping to keep my family together. We got off to a good start, even though he was uncomfortable with the fact that I had a job. I finally convinced him that we needed my income.

For the first few months, Theodore didn't lay a hand on me. I got pregnant again and the abuse started again. This time, I wasn't at all hesitant about leaving.

I had friends like Bertie and Chickee to talk to for moral support. I left Theodore once again and spent the rest of my pregnancy living with my parents. I continued to work until I was eight months pregnant. In fact, my coworkers were all afraid that I was going to give birth right there in the office.

On August 18, 1966, I gave birth to my second son, Jerome La Vonte Young. Andre loved his baby brother from the beginning. He liked to call him "Bubby." After the baby was born, I allowed Theodore to convince me to move back home again. I really wanted my family to be together. That was all that seemed to matter.

My friends were opposed to my decision. They said that I was doing so well on my own. I couldn't get them to realize how much I really just wanted to have a family. My parents and grandparents had families. That's what I wanted, too! So I returned home, only to discover that Theodore had not paid some of the bills, and the gas and phone had been turned off. Still, I was where I felt I belonged.

Once again, we got off to a pretty good start with the new baby. I returned to work, and although Theodore was not working, there were no signs of drug activity around our home. After I had been home for about two months, I got up one morning to begin my normal routine of feeding the boys and getting dressed for work. I fixed Jerome's bottle, then returned to our bedroom to change his diaper. When I pulled back Jerome's blanket, I knew instantly that something was terribly wrong. I turned him over and saw a blood-spotted sheet. The blood had come from his nose. Hysterical, I grabbed him. His head dangled like a loosely filled rag doll.

When I realized that he wasn't moving, I screamed at the top of my lungs. Theodore sprang out of bed and took Jerome from my arms. He administered CPR repeatedly in an effort to revive him. Because we did not have a telephone, I ran barefoot down to the corner telephone booth to call my mother. Within minutes, she arrived to find me crying hysterically. Theodore was clinging to Jerome, saying repeatedly, "He's going to be all right." We quickly jumped in my mom's car and rushed to Bon Air Hospital, where Jerome was pronounced dead on arrival.

The cause of death was pronounced intestinal pneumonia. I wondered how that could be, because just a few days before this occurred, I had taken him to the clinic, and the doctor said that he was a perfectly healthy baby. My whole world went numb when my baby died. I had seen this happen to other people, but I couldn't believe it was happening to me. Despite my numbness, I had the responsibility of preparing for a funeral.

I had never seen such a small casket. Before I knew it, the whole thing was over, and it was time to go home *without* Jerome. Everything seemed so different. Even though Jerome's life was short, his absence left a great emptiness in our home. Andre really missed him. I could tell because he reverted back to asking for the bottle and occasionally wetting his pants. He would look in the crib and call out, "Bubby! Bubby!" For months afterward, I could hear a baby crying in the distance.

One summer afternoon, the guys from the neighborhood gathered outside the house to hang out and shoot the breeze. I was inside doing my usual cleaning and caring for Andre when Theodore came rushing in the house, saying that there had been a fight between two of the neighborhood guys. One of them, Johnnie Doyle, had a reputation for being very headstrong and destructive. The other guy, Joe Brown, was basically a good guy.

Well, after Joe seemed to have given Johnnie all that he could handle, Johnnie had angrily left the scene, threatening to come back and kill him. As I looked out the window, I could see Joe pacing back and forth while the other guys continued their normal activities. Everyone was wondering whether Johnnie would return. After a while, I decided Johnnie was probably just bluffing and went back to my chores and Andre. I walked Andre down the back steps to the backyard. Just as I went back into the house to get my basket of clothes to hang on the line, I heard the distinct sound of a car with loud headers. I knew it had to be Johnnie, because his car was the only one that made that sound. I immediately went back out into the yard to bring Andre inside.

After putting Andre in his room, I ran to the front door to see where Theodore was. Right before I got there, I heard a loud blast that echoed fiercely in my ears. I opened the door to see Johnnie speeding away. I didn't see Theodore. I thought to myself, *Theodore, where are you?*

I didn't holler out. I was trying to remain calm. Then I noticed Joe, lying against the curb. For a few minutes—which seemed like forever—no one said a word. Like a photo, everyone seemed stuck in time. Then, two of the guys dragged Joe to a car and rushed him to the hospital.

I finally spotted Theodore standing in the crowd with several of his friends. Within a few hours, we got the news that Joe had died. I can remember hearing the song "Bumpin' on Sunset," by Wes Montgomery, playing on the radio as if it were a tribute to Joe. For years afterward, I hated to hear that song because it made me believe that something bad was about to happen.

Traumatized by the loss of his son and his friend, Theodore seemed to be on edge. I tried hard to keep him happy.

One day, three of my girlfriends came over to ask me to go to a party. They knew that I needed Theodore's permission. I was reluctant for them to ask for fear he would get angry. One of my girlfriends said, "The hell with this; I'll ask him."

Surprisingly, Theodore agreed. I was still a little reluctant to go, despite the fact that Theodore had consented to it and even encouraged me to go. I should have known that it was really too good to be true.

I smelled trouble. Yet I was so excited about going out with my friends that I didn't think any more about what his motives might have been. I had not been out with my friends in quite some time (or even with Theodore, for that matter). A guy named Tony, who was one of my girlfriend's boyfriend, escorted us. He was not present when Theodore gave me permission to go. I was so excited about going that I didn't give that fact a second thought.

My mother agreed to watch Andre. The stage was set for a wonderful evening.

The party was great, in spite of the fact that I couldn't do any of the new dances. I was eighteen years old and already out of style. I had fun learning the latest steps, even though the dances would probably be different before I got a chance to come out again. After the party, Tony dropped everybody off. When he got to my house, he decided that he wanted to talk with Theodore about something. They knew each other quite well. We picked up Andre from my mom's house and headed to my home.

When we got there, Theodore was lying on the sofa, obviously under the influence of drugs, alcohol, or both. He struggled in vain to get up, although he did manage to raise his head up long enough to say, "I ought to blow your brains out." At that very moment, I realized that I shouldn't have gone and went into the bedroom, preparing for the beating that I knew was coming.

As I heard Tony and Theodore talking, I prayed that Tony would not leave, or that he would at least talk Theodore out of beating me. After I laid Andre down, I went to the closet to hang up his coat. That was when I noticed that the shotgun Theodore kept in the corner of the closet had been tampered with. I immediately put Andre's coat back on him, and stuffed as much of our things as I could carry into a bag. Then I asked Tony to take me back to my mother's house. Theodore was drunk or high and really could not have done much harm to Tony if he'd tried.

Tony gave me his keys and told me to go to his car. He knew that I would be in danger if I stayed. He remained behind to talk to Theodore until he knew I was safely in the car. He ended the conversation, came out to the car, and drove me to my parents' house. Before he left, Tony warned me not to go back to Theodore.

Andre and I had a peaceful night, but the next day all hell broke loose.

I am sure that after Theodore awoke from his intoxicated state, he realized that he had gotten cheated out of the whipping he had planned to give me the night before. That morning, he started calling with threats to beat me if I didn't come home. When I stopped answering the phone, he threatened whoever answered—my mom, dad, or grandmother.

I was determined to be strong. This time, I was not going back. My dream of a wonderful family, being a good wife, and having a loving husband disappeared at that moment.

Theodore began stalking me. I was afraid to go anywhere. When I did go out, I was constantly looking over my shoulder. As much as I hated to, I quit my job because I knew that Theodore would eventually show up there. I did not want to run the risk of being there when he did.

One night after a lot of persuasion from friends, I decided to venture out from my parents' home. Bertie and her boyfriend, Donald, stopped by, and we decided to go for a ride. That's what people did in the sixties when there was nothing else to do. Since Andre was with my mom, I was in no rush to get home. I got into the backseat of Donald's car, and off we went. Donald had a record player in his car, like most cool guys who had cars. He just happened to put on "Bumpin' on Sunset." I told him, "Donald, I'm sorry, but that's my bad-luck song. Every time I've heard it, something bad happens." I asked him to take it off. He just laughed and said, "Aw, Verna! Nothing's going to happen to you. You're with me."

No sooner had we reached the end of the block than we noticed a car speeding straight toward us. The headlights from the approaching car were so bright, I could hardly see. Before we knew what was happening, my car door flew open, and Theodore pulled me out, forcing me into the front seat of his car. Rabbit, one of our friends, was also sitting in the front passenger seat. Theodore jumped in behind me. There I was, sandwiched between the two of them. Theodore looked at me with pure hatred in his eyes and declared, "You will never leave me again."

At that moment, my entire life flashed in front of me. All I could think about was how to keep this from happening. There was no way I was going to go home with him. There was no way I would take a beating from him tonight or ever again. I had to think fast. When Theodore's car came to a stop at the red light at the intersection of Main and Manchester Streets, I noticed that Rabbit seemed to be in deep thought. Perhaps he knew, like I knew, that Theodore would beat me if he ever got me home. Rabbit nervously pushed himself back in the seat as far as he possibly could, giving me the room I needed to jump out.

At that moment, I reached across Rabbit, grabbed the door handle, opened the car door, and slid across his lap in what seemed to be all one motion. Once out of the car, I noticed that an auto parts store called Sopp's was open and ran inside. Theodore swirled his car into the parking lot, coming dangerously close to hitting me. His car was now between the store and me. I quickly ran around the car and into the store. The security officer on duty had seen me run frantically into the store and protectively drew his gun.

Determined to catch me, Theodore ran into the store behind me. At that point, it seemed as if he were driven by foolish blind rage. When the officer ordered him to stop, Theodore challenged him. The officer begged him not to force him to shoot. I stood, shaking with nervous confusion. I wanted him to leave me alone. At the same time, I didn't want to see him hurt. Theodore finally calmed down, and the officer called the police.

I cried because I knew through all of this, Theodore would eventually get me where he wanted me—home and alone. I felt sure that I would get a severe beating and possibly be killed. In those days, police rarely did anything when they were called for domestic disputes. When the police arrived, they decided that it was best for me to go back to my parents' house. They took me there, which was my shelter and refuge. There was no way that

Theodore would show up at my parents' house, acting stupid. But everywhere else I went, he was there, stalking me. There seemed to be no escaping him.

Time and time again, I narrowly escaped running into him. To avoid these constant close calls, I opted to stay at home. In fact, my parents' home became my little prison. Theodore had made so many threats against my family and me that I wasn't even sure if staying home was safe, either. When I did leave home, I was afraid to go alone.

My girlfriends Bertie and Bobbie often came by to comfort me. They would talk about the places that they had been and the fun that they'd had. I was still young and wanted to go out and have fun like they did. But my fear that Theodore would show up was always stronger than my desire to go anywhere.

One day, I got word that the house on 135th Street where I had lived had been raided and that Theodore had been arrested. The feeling I had that day was indescribable. I felt like how I imagined the slaves must have felt when they were told they were free. His arrest was the talk of the neighborhood. The police had actually secured evidence collected during a series of stakeouts. Several other people were booked and jailed, in addition to Theodore, who was the big fish. He was charged with possession with intent to sell and distribute illegal drugs.

After his arrest, I let things cool down for a few days. Then I went to the house to pick up several items that belonged to Andre and me. When I got there, the house didn't look anything like it had when I left it. The police had bashed in both the front and the back doors. The cabinets and drawers were emptied, with the contents strewn all over the floor, and the sofa, chairs, and mattresses were slashed. They had even rolled the carpet up to the middle of the floor.

As I hurriedly gathered our belongings, I couldn't help but think how fortunate I had been that I wasn't there when it all went down.

As I took one last glimpse at the shambles, visions of the misery I had suffered in that house rushed through my mind. I pondered my life with Theodore, the dreams I'd had when we first came here—dreams of a wonderful life with a wonderful man.

We'd had some good times, but we were just children when Theodore was suddenly forced into manhood. That is something that happens to a lot of teenage boys. Some make it through; some don't. Theodore didn't.

SEVEN

Curtis

I DECIDED NOT TO take any time to deal with my sadness. There would be plenty of time to ponder the *whys* and *what ifs* about Theodore and me. But first, it was party time!

By then, I was eighteen years old, living with my parents again, and knew that Andre would be properly cared for when I wasn't home.

Bobbie had just returned home from the Job Corps, and Bertie had dropped out of high school. They became my running buddies.

The three of us were out cruising one day when two cars filled with guys came around the corner. Bertie yelled out to them. They pulled over, and we all talked for a while. Bobbie and Bertie exchanged telephone numbers with some of them. Not me. I was still enjoying my freedom. Within a few weeks, Bertie was dating Donald and Bobbie was dating Mark. They were both guys that we'd met that day.

One night, Andre and I were invited to a beach party with a group of our new friends. I was excited about going because I had never been to a beach party before. I packed Andre's bag, and we went along for what turned out to be an unusually wild experience. I had never been around such crazy-acting people—they talked very loudly, acted stupidly, but were very, very funny. They would talk about each other, and the one being talked about would laugh the hardest, or they would ride down the freeway passing things from one car to the other. I met Curtis Crayon (the brother of Bertie's new boyfriend, Donald) at that beach party. He was one of the funniest people I had ever met.

Everyone hung out in a neighborhood near Manchester at Central Avenue. My mother remembered what I had been through with Theodore, and she thought that I needed to have some fun. I left Andre with my parents so much that people started thinking he was their child.

On many nights, the whole group of us would drink alcohol until we were drunk senseless. Bertie, Bobbie, and I would get to a party any way we could, just so that we could be with our drinking friends. If no one was available to pick us up, we would catch the bus, walk, or occasionally get bold enough to hitchhike in order to be with our friends. The party group seemed to get bigger and bigger, and a relationship began blossoming between Curtis and me.

Our partying included going to clubs. Even though my girlfriends and I were not of age to get into the clubs, a little makeup, fancy hairstyles, and the right clothing got us in without a problem. It was great fun. Our friend Georgia's house would sometimes be the last stop for the evening. We would sleep over, and then wake up, ready to party all over again. This was my life for the next few months.

One night, after coming from a club where Bertie and I had a few too many drinks, I ended up back at Georgia's house. There was a guy there who was interested in me romantically. We were just acquaintances who had known each other for a long time, and I found his persistence extremely irritating. Every time we ran into each other, he started talking the same romantic chatter even though I responded rudely each time. This night was no different.

He started coming on to me at Georgia's house. Since I was wasted, I don't remember this, but everyone present said that I finally exploded at him. I started viciously swinging my fist at him in an attempt to make him leave me alone. In his effort to stop me from hitting him, he accidentally knocked me backward. I fell like a limp rag doll. I happened to be standing in front of the kitchen back door that had a sash window. So when I fell backward, my head crashed through the window. My friends pulled me back through it. The scary part about this incident is that I didn't remember anything after throwing the punches. The next day, everyone who had witnessed this bizarre display told me how lucky I had been.

I finally came to my senses and walked away from the party scene forever. What would happen to Andre if something happened to me? I started staying home and reclaiming my role as Andre's mother. My decision to leave the party scene seemed to be infectious. Curtis soon left the group behind, as did my best friends, Bertie and Bobbie. A few of us had managed to escape a lifestyle that was moving nowhere fast.

With our terrible past behind us, we all started in a more positive direction. I filed for divorce and went to the Neighborhood Youth Corp. to get my job back. Unfortunately, my former position had become automated. In fact, there had been many other changes in NYC procedures that resulted in the loss of traditional jobs.

I was offered a position at the Compton Police Department, which was an NYC-designated company, and began working in the Traffic Division. It was my job to pinpoint accidents on a huge map of the city, as well as file and update the status of tickets.

Because Curtis was mechanically inclined, he landed a part-time position repairing motorcycles at the shop where his dad also worked. Bertie got a job through the Neighborhood Youth Corp. working in the Economic Youth Opportunity Agency (EYOA) office. EYOA, like NYC, was another government-funded agency that assisted youth in finding employment. After Bertie started working at EYOA, she helped me get a job there. My office was one floor above hers.

Bertie and I started saving our money so that we could get ourselves together. At almost nineteen, we felt that we were too grown to live with our parents. After all, we had seen so much from our days on the street; we found living with our parents difficult.

As soon as Bertie and I had finally saved up enough money, we started our search. Our goal was to find a nice place in a good area that was safe and suitable for two young ladies and a small child.

We were rejected a few times because of our age, but we were finally able to find an apartment that we were truly proud of. Our new home was located near the corner of Vermont and Gage Avenues, which was really convenient. We were directly across the street from a Safeway market. A bus stop and shopping center were also within walking distance. The bus dropped us in front of the building where we worked. Bobbie and a few other friends also lived within walking distance.

My greatest challenge was child care. We didn't have a car to transport Andre back and forth to the babysitter who lived across the street from my mom. But my mom, being her usual supportive self, kept Andre during the workweek. She would take him to and from the babysitter and would see to all of his other needs. On weekends, my parents would drop him off at my apartment to spend the weekends with me. I couldn't help but feel guilty about being away from him so much. At the time, there wasn't much that I could do about it. Not long after Bertie and I had completely settled in our apartment, I found out that I was once again pregnant. Curtis handled the news quite well. He was very adamant about giving me money for groceries and other essentials. He would stop by daily on his way from work and would sometimes stay overnight.

Curtis's brother Donald was still dating Bertie. All they did was hang out and drink, which was something I no longer wanted any part of. After Bertie missed a couple of months' rent, she decided to move back home. Curtis and I thought that Bertie's move was for the best because it allowed me to have the apartment all to myself. Curtis agreed to help me financially.

The day after I had cleaned the apartment from top to bottom, Curtis and I went to the movies. When we returned, we noticed a light on. As we approached the door, we heard heavy laughter coming from inside. We also noticed that the screen was not quite attached to the window. When we opened the door, we saw Bertie and Donald sitting on the floor, smoking and drinking Old English 800. Bertie no longer had a key, so she had climbed in through the window. I was so mad that I could have screamed.

I didn't want to lose our friendship, so I decided to give up the apartment and return to my parents' house. I hated to leave such a nice, well-kept place with all of its conveniences, but I felt that this was the best thing to do. Not only that, I had become overwhelmed with guilt about seeing Andre only on the weekends. Moving back home was the best thing for Andre and me. And with a new baby soon to arrive, I could get help from my parents until I was able to get back on my feet. As always, they were there to support me.

My relationship with Curtis continued to blossom. He came and called often. One day, he called me to say that he was in jail. He explained that his sister, Elaine, had asked him to come over to her apartment to do a favor. When he arrived, he found a note on the door, instructing him to go downstairs and wait for her at a neighbor's apartment. When he got down there, Curtis found himself in the midst of a raid. The neighbor was dealing drugs. Everyone in the house went to jail. This was nothing but a case of being in the wrong place at the right time. Curtis wound up being locked up for ninety days. I visited him at the county jail from time to time.

I think that my sudden change from being hardly noticeable to being extra large made my supervisor a little nervous. So I was forced to take leave from my job two months before my baby was due. On my last day at work, the people in the office showered me with so many baby gifts that Bertie and I could barely make it home.

A few days later, I woke up in the morning feeling kind of strange. I had planned to visit Curtis and then go to L.A. General Hospital. As I was preparing to leave, Bertie dropped by on her way to work. I dressed Andre and took him across the street to the babysitter and then headed to the bus stop with Bertie. Bertie's stop came first. I went on to my second bus alone.

When I arrived at the jail, I filled out a visit form and stood in line to submit it. While doing that, I felt a slight pain. I asked the lady behind me to save my place in line while I went to get a drink of water. When I got back, there were only a few people in front of me. I had only been back in line a few minutes when I felt another pain. Determined to follow through with my plans for seeing Curtis before going to the hospital, I got out of line, walked until the pain subsided, and returned. Now there was only one person ahead of me. I managed to turn my visitor's slip in and sit down for a hot second before a stronger pain hit me. At that point, I knew that it was time to go.

I headed over to the administration building to call a taxi; however, my labor pains were so strong that I couldn't even talk. Because they came too fast to bear, I went to lie down on a bench inside the building. A lady who walked by and saw me lying there stopped to ask if I was all right. When she realized that I was in labor, she frantically ran for help. She returned with her brother-in-law. He got me up and hurriedly, but carefully, walked me outside the building toward the parking lot. As we walked, I became weak at the knees and slumped to the ground. In a desperate attempt to keep me from falling, the man scooped me up in his arms and ran to the car. After carefully placing me in the backseat, he sat next to me, trying his best to comfort me as the lady drove hastily toward the hospital. At one point, she made a wrong turn, which led us into an area of warehouses and trucking yards. Every time I would moan, she got more and more nervous. Within minutes, we were back on the main street. As luck would have it, a police officer was traveling in the opposite direction. The lady jumped out of her car, flagged down the officer, and told him what the problem was. She then jumped back in the car and followed the police car, with sirens blaring, all the way to the hospital.

When we arrived, the lady's brother-in-law ran into the emergency room, carrying me in his arms. After I was admitted, a red blanket was thrown over me. I was whisked up to the delivery room, bypassing all of the bleeding, moaning, and desperately ill patients in the emergency waiting room. Before the lady and her brother-in-law could even leave the hospital, I gave birth to a baby boy. Because it was an emergency, no one stopped to take the names of the persons who brought me to the hospital. To this day, I do not know who those people were.

Tyree Du Sean Crayon was born March 19, 1968. He was two months premature and weighed only four pounds, eleven ounces. He could not be released from the hospital until he weighed five pounds. Upon my release from the hospital, my father picked me up. When I got home, all I wanted to do was lie down. In addition to hurting physically, I felt depressed about not being able to bring Tyree home. After I had finally managed to get a few hours of sleep, an excruciating abdominal pain suddenly woke me up. My mom prepared to rush me back to the hospital. The car would not start, so we had to call Uncle Dave, my mom's big brother, who lived close by.

Although I saw Uncle Dave often, he was sure a sight for sore eyes that night, given all the pain I was in. I felt every bump, every turn, and every stop; I felt them all, right in the pit of my stomach, as we rode. I felt my body temperature rising rapidly. The pain was actually worse than the labor pains. I was thinking all sorts of wild thoughts. *Was there still another baby in me? Did they release me too soon?* I even thought I was going to die!

When we finally arrived at the hospital, my temperature was 104 degrees. I was rushed into the examination room. I could hear the nurse trying to calm down my crying mother. The examination revealed that the doctors had failed to remove the afterbirth when they delivered Tyree. They rushed me into surgery to repair the problem. Relieved from the pain, I was finally able to go to sleep.

After several days of recovery, I felt like I had been given a new lease on life. I did not like being in the hospital and was quite eager to leave. I had been told that it still would be a few more days before I could take Tyree home. I truly hated the thought of leaving my baby there again.

At home, Andre was waiting anxiously to meet his new brother. My mom had already explained to him that he would soon have a new playmate. Waiting to pick up baby Tyree took only a few days, but it seemed to take a lifetime for the day to arrive when we could bring him home from the hospital. He was quite small, but he seemed to be very strong. We felt confident that he would be all right.

When we got home, Andre thought his new playmate would be able to play immediately. He was so excited that he ran to get his favorite ball and prepared to toss it to Tyree. I explained to him that the baby had to get a little bit bigger before he could play. He was a tad bit disappointed at first. I remedied that by giving him "big brother duties," such as assisting with changing diapers, feedings, and occasionally holding him. I was fortunate because the hospital staff had already gotten Tyree on a regular sleeping and eating schedule.

As I cared for this new little boy, the memory of Jerome's death caused me to focus on whether Tyree was still breathing. After a while, I became comfortable that he was healthy, so I stopped my constant checking. Yet, after losing a baby, I don't think I ever became completely at ease with my child's health.

When Tyree was about two months old, I prepared to go back to work. Andre's sitter agreed to keep both boys. All I needed to do was find a job.

Bertie, who was consistently checking on me to make sure all was well, came by to let me know that she had gotten a new job at Pacific Telephone and Telegraph Company. I wanted to work there also. She obtained the job through the EYOA, but that program had ended. I went directly to the Pacific Telephone and Telegraph Company's employment office, filled out an application, and took the employment test.

I passed the test with flying colors and was hired as a compilation clerk. I was responsible for associating bills with all the necessary forms and preparing them for mailing. Even though I had only a ninth-grade education, I was smart. In fact, many people didn't know that I had not finished high school, and I didn't tell them anything different. I was a very good employee and was promoted as soon as my ninety-day probation had ended. It was a wonderful feeling working on my first *real* job and doing well at it.

Because I had a good-paying job, I was able to become more independent. My goal was to get my own place and create a new life for myself and my boys. Andre was a little guy who seemed to have grown-up sense. Sometimes I believe I pushed him beyond normal limits. Like my mother had with me, I didn't allow Andre to say, "I can't." By the time he was ready for school, I had taught him so much. He knew the entire alphabet, how to count to one hundred, his address and telephone number, how to spell and write his own name, and how to tell time on the hour. He had even learned how to tie his shoes.

When Curtis got out of jail, his brother planned a coming-home party. Early that morning, his friend Edgar Moton came over to the house to see if we wanted to go with him to pick up Curtis. We all packed into the car and rode to the L.A. County Jail. To our surprise, Curtis had already been released and was apparently on his way home by bus. I asked Moton to take me home so I could be there when Curtis returned.

After I arrived home, Curtis called to say that he was out of jail and had talked to Moton. He advised me not to get in the car with Moton because it was stolen. Little did he know that the kids and

I had already been in the car. I was amazed that Moton, a friend of the family, would put the kids and me in that kind of danger. I assured Curtis that I would not get in the car with Moton again.

When Moton returned to take us to the party, I told him that I wasn't ready to go, and that I would get there later. Curtis must have spent most of the morning seeing friends and family members. Later that afternoon, we got to see him, and he spent the rest of the day with us. That night, we joined our friends and family members at the party. I noticed a change in Curtis. He wasn't really into the party. Maybe being in jail had made a difference. After a little bit of partying, Curtis was ready for us to go. His friends begged him to stay, but it seemed that being with the kids and me was more important to him than anything else. After leaving the party, we stopped at a store to buy some food, which included treats for Andre and Tyree. We then went to a motel room, where we stayed for the rest of the weekend. We spent a lot of time talking about how we were going to make a better life together.

First thing on Monday morning, Curtis went out looking for a job. He was fortunate to find work right away. Once everything began to fall into place, we began to make wedding plans. We started by selecting the wedding party. I asked Bertie to be my maid of honor and Sharon, a new good friend from work, to be my bridesmaid. Curtis's brother Donald was to be his best man, and his good friend Mark was his groomsman. Andre was the ring bearer. Taffy-lon, my previous supervisor's daughter, was the flower girl. I made the two ladies' and the flower girl's dresses. My dress was custom-made. Because I tended to be somewhat flamboyant in the way I dressed, the design of my wedding dress was quite unique.

Curtis and I managed to save some money to buy furniture. We anticipated getting additional items that we needed for our home as wedding gifts. Our biggest challenge was finding a nice, affordable apartment in which to live.

On my wedding day, Curtis, Donald, and Mark were an hour late. As we all sat around waiting for them, Sharon helped take the edge off of everything with her humor. At one point, she said, "Don't worry, Verna. One monkey don't stop no show." Because she kept us laughing and joking the whole time, the hour passed fairly quickly. When the guys finally showed up, all of them, including Curtis, were drunk from partying all night.

Curtis's parents, who were always late, showed up with a movie camera just in time to film the tail end of the wedding. The reception was at their home. After we left the chapel, we headed there for the reception. Their home was beautifully decorated. The Crayons were very proud of their home and took pride in keeping it looking nice.

After the reception at the Crayons', one of our friends had an after party. Curtis and I stopped by briefly. When we got there, the Isley Brothers' hit song "It's Your Thing" was playing. It was also playing when we left, although I don't recall if it played the whole time we were there. I was so happy; nothing else mattered. I had a family again.

My parents agreed to allow us to stay at their house until we found our own apartment. It took us about two weeks to find a place of our own. It was a nice, small apartment on Eighty-first, between Figueroa and Hoover, in Los Angeles. Curtis's grandmother let us use her car until we could afford to buy our own. I caught the bus to work, while Curtis used the car to get to his job. Getting to work by bus for him was more difficult. With the support of our family and our working together, the marriage got off to a really good start. We were able to purchase new furniture and open a bank account, and had the opportunity to use our wonderful wedding gifts. Things were working well. I was truly happy again.

As a parent, I was very strict. I made sure that Andre and Tyree were well behaved. I wanted them to be near perfect. Even though they tried really hard, they couldn't always live up to my standards of perfection. When they did not, I had no problem punishing them. Tyree especially was always getting into some kind of difficulty. Andre, on the other hand, would generally stay out of trouble.

We had lots of good times together. I took excellent care of my kids and performed all of my wifely duties. Curtis was a very loving and caring husband and dad, although at times he got a little controlling. When that would occur, I was reminded of the abuse I had experienced with Theodore. Although I did not think Curtis could ever be as violent as Theodore, I had promised myself that I would never let anyone treat me like that ever again. When Curtis became controlling, I took a very defiant attitude, which led to some knock-down, drag-out arguments.

Because we were one of the few couples in our circle of friends who had a place of our own, people came over frequently. The constant company eventually became a problem for me because I found it difficult to get up in the morning after entertaining friends until the early morning hours. At times, after they left, Curtis and I argued until the wee hours of the morning, usually over little or nothing.

One evening, Curtis and I had an argument that turned so violent that I decided to take my children and leave. As I headed for the door, he grabbed my arm, causing me to lose my balance. As I fell, I struck my eye on the corner of a heavy marble table. Needless to say, I was too hurt to leave that night.

The next morning, I awoke to find my left eye and the whole side of my face badly swollen. I couldn't go to work looking battered, but I had already been late and absent a few too many times. The telephone company had strict policies about too much absenteeism and tardiness. I tried to think of a good excuse for missing work so that I would not risk losing my job. I decided to tell my supervisor that my father had died. By the next day, flowers began arriving from my coworkers, and we got sympathy calls from people.

I was dismissed when they found out that I had lied. I felt bad that the lie got so out of hand. I also felt badly about using my father as an excuse.

In an instant, we turned into a one-income household, and things started to get a little tough. Being at home did allow me to spend more time with the children. But I needed a job because we needed the additional money. I convinced myself that it wasn't the end of the world and that we could get through this rough spot. Then I found out that I was pregnant again.

The stress from arguing and fighting with Curtis took its toll on me. As a result, I delivered another premature baby, this time in my sixth month. We named him Curtis Alexander Crayon II.

Because his lungs were not fully developed, he was unable to breathe properly, and he died two days later.

We barely had enough income to pay our bills and purchase our necessities because I still wasn't working. Shortly after the baby died, we were forced to move to a less expensive place on Parmelee Street, near Central Avenue and Imperial Highway. I hoped that the move would be temporary because I didn't think that the area was fit for raising two young children. It was located near a housing project.

Not long after the move, I began pounding the pavement in search of another job. Once again, God was looking out for me. During my job search, I answered a want ad for a position in the credit department at Sears and Roebuck. I filled out the necessary paperwork, took a test, and was hired immediately.

EIGHT

Work

DIANE, THE GIRLFRIEND of one of Curtis's friends, agreed to babysit Andre and Tyree. Her house was conveniently on the way to my new job. Each morning, Curtis dropped the kids and me off at Diane's house on his way to work. I would have time for a quick nap, after which I would freshen up and leave to catch the bus to my new job.

My job as a credit correspondent was a good experience. I worked with a group of very interesting co-workers, and I also met an array of interesting customers. At the end of each day, I left with the feeling that I could do any job in the company. I soaked up all the knowledge that I could and enjoyed my work very much. But I only kept this job for approximately six months.

During the first few months that Diane began keeping the boys, I noticed that Andre was extremely hungry when we got home, and that Tyree had severe diaper rash. This seemed odd because I always left plenty of food, snacks, and diapers with Diane. I concluded that she obviously was not doing a good job of babysitting my children. I needed a babysitter in order to continue working. Finding out that the person that we had chosen was not doing a good job presented a real problem.

One day, I looked in Diane's cabinets and found that all of the food I had been bringing for the boys was piled high. I confronted her about what I had found. She agreed to do better. But my mind was already made up. At that point, I immediately began to search for another babysitter.

I soon learned that all of the Sears credit files were being sent to the new office located in Torrance. I also found out that computers would perform my job. Although Sears offered everyone in my department the opportunity to transfer to the new location, it was simply too far for me to travel by bus. Sears offered several people who could not transfer the option of different positions at the present location, based on seniority, but I wasn't one of them because I had not been working there long enough. The remainder of us were laid off, and, considering my child-care issues, I really didn't mind. For a little while at least, I would have the opportunity to stay home with Andre and Tyree. I vowed that before I would seek employment again, my first priority would be to find a reliable babysitter.

Although I enjoyed staying at home, my not working meant that we had money problems once again. What little savings we did have quickly whittled away. We were forced to uproot once again. I didn't mind leaving the apartment, but I was certain that if we couldn't afford where we were, we surely couldn't afford anything better. We ended up in a one-bedroom apartment on Eighty-second Street, between Figueroa and Hoover. I hoped that this move would be temporary and that things would turn around for us soon.

Our first day on Eighty-second Street, I noticed three little girls at an apartment across the street who looked familiar. I learned that they were my cousin Lois's daughters. I was pleasantly surprised to find that I had relatives living directly across the street. And, ironically, my friend Bobbie moved next door to Lois in a duplex that she shared with another friend, Shirley. My sister-in-law Elaine also moved down the street with her family. Knowing so many people in the community was very comforting.

I soon became the neighborhood babysitter. I also took care of my brother-in-law's children, Pookie and Yvette, for nine months while their mother was in jail. Sometimes I would babysit Curtis's youngest brother, Daryl, who was Andre's age. Our apartment seemed to be a haven for kids. At times, there would be so many kids in the house that I had to be sure to count them all when I called them in to eat.

In addition to caring for children, sewing also became a source of income for me, just as it had been for my mother and grandmother. My new sewing customers helped to supplement my unemployment benefits.

When the time finally came for Andre to start school, both he and I were excited. I made plans to sew all of his clothes. He was going to be the best-dressed boy in the whole school. I started sewing over the summer so that by the time school started, all of his clothes would be ready to wear. In those days, vests and pantsuits were the "in thing." In addition to sewing for Andre, I also sewed dresses for my niece Yvette. I made sure that they all dressed nicely for school. Pookie wore good clothing that Andre had outgrown.

I would get the cloth from a small fabric store on Vermont Avenue. Then I would select from remnant pieces of fabric in a wide array of colors. I spent hours making different styles of clothing. I made so many clothes that Andre was able to wear a different pantsuit to school every day. I always received compliments from the teacher and even other parents about how well dressed Andre was. The compliments from other people made us both very proud. The teachers also complimented us on how well disciplined he was.

Andre was an all-around excellent student. My being home with him so much in the beginning gave him a jump-start academically. It also helped Andre realize how much I really loved him, which gave him confidence to go out to face the new world of strange people at school. He always received good grades, quickly earning the respect of his teachers.

Once he got settled in school, I was still faced with the issue of our living conditions. We didn't live on Eighty-second Street for very long, but it was long enough to see lots of dramas and have sad memories. For instance, a pair of women who were drug addicts lived there. They often stumbled down the street. And in one of the apartments across the street from us, the owner had converted a small recreation room into a neighborhood nightclub, which drew its share of characters. We also had a host of women, whom I called the "county (welfare) women," staying in nearby housing. These women had men who hung around them only at or near the first and fifteenth of each month. In addition to these things, a lot of children gathered outside to play. Some of them were bad, and some of their parents were even worse.

One day, I watched two kids who were approximately three years old get into a little scuffle. The mothers got into an argument about whose child hit who first. Their solution to the problem was to meet outside, armed with knives, and fight it out themselves. While they fought, the two kids had made up and gone back to playing. Afterward, the mothers forbade the kids from playing together ever again. As I witnessed this encounter from my window, I recalled thinking what a wonderful world this would be if adults could resolve their differences the way kids do. Andre and Tyree played with the children that I babysat, so I didn't have to worry about getting into an altercation with neighborhood moms.

One morning, I got the sad news that my grandmother on my mom's side had passed away. I cried so much that day when I thought about my grandmother being gone. She was eighty-three years old, but I guess I expected her to live forever. The day of her funeral was one of the saddest days of my life. I still miss her so much.

The night after the funeral, the shaking of my bed woke me up. Then I felt what seemed like a cold hand on my back, attempting to keep me from rising. When I got up, I looked to see if Andre or Tyree had gotten into bed with me, but I found them fast asleep. As I gazed out of the bedroom door, I saw an image in pink go past. I remembered that my grandmother was wearing pink as she lay in the casket. A creepy feeling suddenly came over me. I knew I couldn't leave the house because the kids were asleep. I didn't know where I would go anyway. I couldn't go back to sleep, so I went outside to sit on the porch until Curtis returned home from his mother's house.

For several months after that, I would occasionally feel the bed moving. I simply got used to it, and I never mentioned it to Curtis. I wondered if he ever felt the bed moving, too. But since he never mentioned anything about it, I just kept it to myself. At first, it was frightening because there was no explanation as to why this was happening. I finally concluded that my grandmother was just checking on me, as she would often do when she lived at my parents' house.

When I was younger, she would come into my bedroom and warmly and softly touch my back. This made me feel safe, secure, and loved. Sometimes when she came in, I wouldn't move, even though I knew she was there. I would just smile to myself, enjoying the fact she was there for me.

At this point in my life, I had become a homebody, wife, and mother. Besides my children and sewing, the only other interest that I had was music. I had a phenomenal record collection. Music was always playing in the house. I cleaned house to music. I had my best thoughts while listening to music. And I lived by certain words from certain songs. When people dropped by, they sometimes thought that there was a party going on. But it was just the boys, my music, and me. After Andre learned how to play the records, I would occasionally let him deejay for me and for our company. Even then, he was really good. Andre learned to recognize record labels even before he could read by looking at the color of the label or other distinguishing features.

One day as I was getting ready to go to the fabric store, Bobbie and Shirley, two friends who lived across the street, stopped by to advise me that there was a new retail store called National Dollar opening on Vermont, near Manchester. They were both planning to apply for jobs there and wanted me to join them. I told them that I would walk with them since I was going that way. Once we got to the new store, they convinced me to stop there with them to complete an application, after which I went to the fabric store. No sooner had I gotten home than I received a call from the store manager, offering me an interview. I was so excited that I ran across the street to tell Bobbie and Shirley that I'd received a call about the position and to see if they had received one as well. They had not. At that very moment, I remembered some advice that my mother had given me— "Never take a friend with you when you're applying for a job; the friend may get the job, and you may not." I went in for an interview and was immediately hired. Shirley and Bobbie were a little upset because they were the ones really looking for a job. They got over it eventually and were very happy for me. Even though neither of them received a call, Shirley continued to try to get a job there and was eventually hired. Bobbie searched for jobs at other places.

My new employment was not totally good news to some of my other friends because it meant that they would have to find someone else to watch their children. It was really bittersweet for me because I truly loved watching children. However, I couldn't afford to pass up more money. My new job was within walking distance from home, and my hours were the opposite of Curtis's, so we didn't even need a babysitter to watch the boys.

Now that we had a little more income coming into the household, we thought it was time to look for a bigger place in a better environment. We were able to find a place nearby on Eighty-third

Street, between Hoover and Vermont. It was a nice, roomy three-bedroom back house (a house in back of a small house). Later, I was concerned that we had settled on a place too soon. Shirley moved into the apartment building next door to our house. We both thought that this was a better neighborhood, but that proved not to be true. During the first three months, Shirley's house was burglarized three times. We were fortunate not to get hit because either Curtis or I was always home. But we were concerned because the bigger kids that lived in the front house always picked fights with Andre and Tyree. And there was a group of undesirable people that were constantly hanging around. Eventually, Shirley and I both bought guns for our protection.

I continued to walk to and from work, but that soon became a problem because of the roving gangs of youth. One night when I had almost reached home, a car drove up beside me, and two guys demanded that I throw them my purse. Without hesitation, I pulled out my gun and aimed it at them. They sped away. I waited until they were out of sight before running home so they wouldn't see where I lived. I knew then that we would have to move, so I immediately began making plans.

The final straw came when I returned home one evening to find that my house had been burglarized while Curtis and the boys had gone shopping. Besides that, I was totally fed up with living in other people's properties. I wanted us to find a home of our own. I began exploring the possibility of buying a house where my kids could have their own yard, and we could have peace of mind.

We didn't have any money saved, but I was still determined to become a homeowner. So I started saving the money that I made from sewing and other odd jobs until I had enough to meet each of the requirements (down payment and closing costs) to purchase the home for my family. At a young age, I had accomplished what took my parents many years to do. I felt that I could do anything. I had come a long way from those high school days filled with bad decisions. We were now adults who made grown-up decisions. I felt good about the whole thing.

Our new house was located on Imperial Highway, a few blocks from Central Avenue. Andre, who was seven years old, transferred to the school in that area. Our old faithful babysitter, who lived across the street from my parents' house, once again agreed to watch the boys. I taught Andre how to catch the bus from school to the babysitter's house. Shortly after the move, I was transferred to the National Dollar store at the El Segundo and Avalon location, which was closer to my mother and the babysitter.

One day, the babysitter called me at work to say that Andre hadn't made it in from school. I left work frantic, thinking the worst. I got a ride to my parents' house, and we went out searching for Andre. After a few hours of looking everywhere that we thought he might be, we stopped back by the babysitter's house to find that Andre was there. He told us that a man had taken him away from the bus stop and gave us a description of the man. We went looking for the stranger, but upon further questioning, Andre finally admitted he had gone off with a friend to play at a nearby park. This was so unlike him. He always followed instructions very well and had never done anything except what was expected of him. But like any child, he could sometimes do wrong, as I had to realize. I gave him a sermon about how bad things can happen to kids who wander off. He got the same lecture from my parents and the babysitter, too. He saw how upset we were and promised to never do that again.

Andre finished the year at school with no more problems. The following school year, we transferred him to Mark Twain Elementary School, which was within walking distance from the babysitter's house. I had a lot more peace of mind knowing that he could walk to and from school with the kids in my parents' neighborhood. Andre continued to get good grades throughout his years in elementary school. We established a new transportation plan whereby I would catch the bus with Andre and Tyree in the mornings to the babysitter's house and walk one block to the shopping center where my job was located. When my mom got home in the evening, she would go across the street, get Andre and Tyree, and take them to her house. By the time I got off work, my mom had already let them play, fed them dinner, and made sure that Andre had done his homework. When I arrived, we would all catch the bus from my mom's house to go home.

It was a challenging time, but as a young, struggling mother, I did what I had to do. I don't think I ever thought it was tough at the time. I was determined to do well someday.

Looking back, I wonder sometimes how I made it through the trying times. My mom always says, "Life is not a bed of roses. You have to see some bad times in order to recognize the good times. If life was all good, you wouldn't recognize the good."

NINE

Divorce and Reconciliation

AFTER SEVERAL YEARS of stable employment, Curtis lost his job. I didn't know the reason, and he didn't want to talk about it. Curtis's unemployment led once again to marital discord. We argued and fought often. We had come so close to making it work and then this happened. Curtis started spending a lot of time away from home, hanging out with friends, drinking, and doing drugs. After one too many arguments, I decided to ask for a divorce. Curtis was not happy at all about my decision.

Curtis was a good-hearted man who was always there for the kids and me. I could deal with his drinking because I drank occasionally. But I couldn't handle his drug use. I had always heard about how difficult it is to get a person off drugs after they are hooked. I didn't want to drag my kids or myself through that for

Curtis or any other man. Although Curtis had not become a habitual user, I felt he was well on his way to becoming one. Most of his friends drank and used drugs. Whenever he was with them, he would come home high.

He promised to stop using drugs and limit his visits with friends if the kids and I returned home. I decided to give him another chance. So we moved back. But the arguments and fights continued. I asked him to leave. I had called my mom to come and get us before the argument became physical. My mom went to talk to him to let him know that she was taking me and the kids to her house until he cooled off. She searched the house and then went to the backyard and discovered that he had locked himself in the garage and was sitting in the car with the windows rolled up and the engine running. Mama told me to call the fire department because it appeared that he was trying to commit suicide. While I searched for the phone number, Mama went back outside and talked Curtis out of the car. If he cared so little about his own life to want to end it, how could I trust him with my children's lives or mine? I was totally fed up and filed for a divorce.

Under the divorce decree, I was awarded custody of the kids and the house. I attempted to go on with my life. Curtis continued to harass me with threats of violence to the point that I finally took out a restraining order against him. I couldn't handle paying for a house where I couldn't live comfortably. And although I hated to, I had to walk away. However, since I had come from strong stock, I was convinced that I would be bent, but not broken. My grandparents had made it. My parents made it. And I was going to make it, too!

I immediately began to look for an apartment for the boys and me. Bobbie told me about a new apartment complex that was in the final stages of construction. She and I both applied for one of the units. While waiting for the apartment to be completed, the kids and I lived with my parents. I was able to save money and develop a new survival plan for my family. The apartment complex, which was gated and guarded, was located in the city of Compton, at the corner of Laurel Street and Wilmington Avenue. When it was first built, it was a safe environment for the kids and me. Our apartment had three bedrooms, so both boys could have their own room. Andre and Tyree still chose to share a bedroom because they wanted to be close to one another. We used the other bedroom as a den to entertain company.

I always kept a clean house, and I taught Andre and Tyree to do likewise. Even as little boys, I gave them chores. Andre felt he was the man of the house at a very young age. Although he was too young to take on all the responsibilities of a man, he did his best to look out for us. If someone entered our home that he didn't feel comfortable with, he would remain close by me until the person was gone. I laid down very strict rules for my sons regarding manners, appearance, and their education. I expected nothing less than the best from them in whatever they did.

Though I had many male friends, I was not intimate with any of them at this point. I wanted to be a good mother. My friends came by quite frequently, but only when they had something to give us. I guess they realized that I truly was a struggling mother, one determined to get ahead, even if it meant struggling by myself. My number-one goal in life was to *succeed.*

One of my friends would come over almost every Friday to take me to the record store. He knew I loved music. Because of his generosity, I had the largest record collection of all my friends. My refrigerator stayed full of juices, sodas, and milk. Friends would bring beer and wine for themselves and to share with me.

Bobbie moved into the same apartment complex soon after we did. Her apartment was adjacent to ours. She was the single parent of a daughter named Valissa. We looked out for one another. We visited each other frequently.

After a while, I grew tired of having company every night because I missed spending time alone with Andre and Tyree. Eventually, I sometimes resorted to not answering the door when friends came by. I would look through the peephole first. If it wasn't my mom or dad, I did not answer the door.

One evening after work, I walked to my parents' house. I was thinking about asking my mom to watch the boys for me because my friends had asked me to go to a party. Because I had not gone out in a while, I really wanted to accept the offer. Mom agreed to watch the boys and even offered to drive me home instead of my taking the bus.

My dad and the boys rode with us so that they could accompany my mom back home. I sat in the front seat with Mom, while Dad sat in the backseat with Andre and Tyree. As we approached the corner of Wilmington and Laurel Street, Mom inched up to the middle of the intersection to make a left turn onto Laurel Street. When the light turned red for the oncoming traffic, she proceeded to make her turn. At that moment, I saw a car speeding toward us like a bat out of hell. I started yelling, "Mama!

Mama! Mama!" as I braced myself for the impact. The car crashed into us with such force that we spun around and landed on the curb on the opposite side of the street. My first instinct was to check to see if everyone was okay. Mom appeared to be a little shaken and disoriented, but was unharmed. Dad was okay, too. I could hear Tyree frantically screaming the whole time, but I couldn't tell whether he was hurt or just scared. As I was making sure that he wasn't hurt, I looked to make sure Andre was all right. When I scanned the car, I didn't see him. I jumped out of the car, frantically yelling out to him. A police officer arrived on the scene immediately and pulled Andre out from under the seat. I was hysterical when I saw that my child had blood all over his face and wasn't moving.

Andre had gone to sleep with his head against the window. The impact of the crash threw him to the other side of the car. The broken glass from the window cut several gashes in his face. Tyree suffered a minor cut to the back of his head. The officer didn't wait for an ambulance. Instead, he put me, Andre, and Tyree in the patrol car and rushed us to the hospital. The nearest hospital for trauma victims was Dominguez Valley Hospital. My mom and dad remained at the scene to exchange information with the driver of the other vehicle and the police.

I called Bobbie, who picked up my parents to bring them to the hospital. Andre was in terrible pain. As his mother, I felt every bit of it. He acted very mature, however, as a doctor stitched up the gashes on his face. I was happy he was not more seriously injured, but I prayed that the cuts would not leave permanent scars. Thank God, we were all able to go home that night.

I got the boys settled in bed for the night, knowing they probably would not sleep well. Then I sat around a while, talking with Bobbie and my parents back at our apartment. I was reminded that night what a wonderful friend Bobbie was. She was always there for me, just as I was for her. I had forgotten all about the party. Instead, I spent the night watching Andre and Tyree. Bobbie drove my parents home.

It had been a year since I had seen Curtis. I called him the next day to let him know what had happened. He wanted to make sure the boys were okay. Although I didn't need any more drama in my life, I thought that it was only right that I allow him to see them under the circumstances. I recalled also that the restraining order was still in effect. I weighed the situation and finally decided that a father should be allowed the privilege of seeing his kids at a time like this.

After that day, Curtis began visiting regularly. The boys were always so happy to see their daddy that I didn't complain about the fact that he was violating the restraining order. After Andre began to complain about pain in his chest and I noticed that he had begun to favor one side after the accident, Curtis and I decided to take him to a doctor.

Curtis's family's doctor, Dr. Anderson, examined Andre. An X-ray diagnosed a broken collarbone. The X-rays that were taken the night of the accident were said to have been clear. Later, I received a letter that stated that after a more thorough check, they found abnormalities. Under Dr. Anderson's watch, however, Andre got the best possible care for his injury.

He handled the pain from his injury so well. I wondered if that was because I had taught him the importance of enduring pain when he complained about simple aches and pains from small cuts and bruises. Or maybe it was Andre's nature to remain cool and calm under pressure. That personality trait has been his trademark to this day.

As Curtis's visits continued, he began hinting about us getting back together. I was very reluctant to do so because I had really gotten used to the peace of mind of not constantly fussing and fighting. There was no way that I wanted to put the boys and myself through that again. I must admit that we could have used Curtis's financial help. In those days, it was difficult to collect child support, and I didn't even try. When people divorced, they went on their merry way. At times, we were so strapped for cash that I would search between the cushions and empty out my purses, searching for change to buy dinner.

Curtis eventually convinced me to take him back. He had to do a lot of talking, begging, pleading, and promising that he would do the right thing before I agreed to it. I finally consented to try it again. I was scared to death—not for my safety, but that we would fail again. While I was on my own, I managed to buy new furniture for the boys' room and the living room. I had also placed a dining room set and bar in layaway. As his first gesture of goodwill, Curtis got the dining room set and bar out of layaway.

Our apartment looked like a picture out of an interior-decorating magazine. The living room and kitchen were nicely decorated with white furniture trimmed in black with red accents. The master bedroom had a round blue-velvet headboard and footstool against a round waterbed. People often wondered how I managed to keep everything so neat with small children. They just didn't know that

Andre and Tyree were exactly like their mother. They, too, had grown to like nice things. I felt that having children should not deny a person the privilege of having nice things. After all, our having nice things at home taught the boys to respect other people's nice things.

Curtis and I got along wonderfully for a while, except for the fact that he constantly asked me to consider remarrying him, a subject that I kept evading. Marriage always seemed to be where my problems started. As a woman, I think I expected too much from marriage. And, as a result, I made some bad decisions. I didn't want to go through that again. So we continued to live together, unmarried.

TEN

My Accident and My Education

W E SPENT A lot of time doing things as a family. We went on camping trips with Curtis's parents to Lake Isabella and Salton Sea. His parents took care of all the details for the trips, such as choosing the date and reserving the trailers and campsites.

When we first began going on the trips, our group consisted of my family, Curtis's parents, his younger brother Daryl, his sister, Elaine, her family, his brother Donald, and his family. As time went on, the trips became popular, and other friends and family members joined us for the fun.

Curtis's dad rode a motorcycle and was a member of a club called the L.A. Rattlers. Once a year, many of the motorcycle clubs in the United States held a large gathering at what was called the Salton Sea Run. Each year we looked forward to going down to Salton Sea for the event. There were hundreds of fine bikes and lots of beautiful people. It was exciting to see the variety of motorcycle clubs with their members wearing sharp jean vests and leather jackets with the clubs' names on the back. Everyone sat proudly on their bikes, rolling down the highway two by two. It seemed as if the long parade of bikes owned the road. I loved hearing the sound of the cycles as they entered the campsite. To me, it sounded like a continuous roar of thunder, coupled with the beat of a bass drum. What club members called the "heavy throttle" shook the earth beneath my feet like a small earthquake. The constant roar was in the air all weekend. The air was also filled with loud conversations and heavy laughter.

I remember one Salton Sea trip in the summer of 1975. We all loaded up in cars, vans, a camper, and a pickup truck that carried our bikes and the cases of beer, which Curtis's dad always provided. When we arrived, we began our usual routine of unpacking the cars, organizing things in our trailers, and getting the kids bedded down. The adults stayed up to enjoy the rest of the night, laughing, talking, and drinking until one by one, everyone eventually went to bed.

The next morning, Curtis's brother Donald discovered that he had lost his keys, possibly at the gas station where we had stopped on the way. He and his wife, Hithia, decided to ride one of the motorcycles back to the gas station to search for the keys. Curtis followed them on another motorcycle. He asked me to go with him. I refused at first because I had a lot to do to prepare the campsite. After much prodding, I finally agreed.

The ride was wonderful. I enjoyed the morning air blowing through my hair and the wind in my face. *This is the life,* I thought to myself. I believe we were going about ninety miles an hour when, suddenly, Donald saw a bunch of bikers at a roadside stop and decided he wanted to turn off the highway to join them. The road was a two-lane highway. Instead of signaling that he was going to turn, Donald sped ahead of us and turned directly in front of us. We had two choices. We could either make the sudden turn with him or go around into the oncoming lane, smack into a diesel truck. As Donald completed the turn, he stopped to see if we were still with him. We made the turn right behind him. Because he stopped, we were forced to plow right into him as we came out of the turn. I immediately flew off the bike and into the air. I don't remember much of what happened beyond that point, but I do recall that after I slid, rolled, and flipped, I ended up at the bottom of a ditch. I may have lost consciousness for a few seconds. But then I slowly regained my hearing, sight, and feelings. I could hear people asking if I was all right. When my vision began to clear up, I could see people standing around me. By the looks on their faces, it seemed that I was hurt pretty badly. After the feeling returned to my body, I was in excruciating pain.

Hithia, Donald, and Curtis were also hurt, although not as badly as I was. After the paramedics arrived, we were taken through the winding mountain roads to the nearest hospital in a small town called Indio, California. The trip seemed to take forever, probably because I was in so much pain. When we arrived, I was rushed directly to the emergency room to begin treatment for my injuries. I suffered a laceration to the forehead and asphalt burns to my left thigh and arm. Anyone who has ever had an asphalt burn knows it can feel more painful than a fire burn. I had gravel embedded in my left thigh and arm, which had to be removed piece by piece. Lord knows what a truly painful experience that was to endure. The denim from my jeans, which was also embedded in my skin, had to be scrubbed out. More pain. To me, getting burned is just as bad as being in labor, as far as the level of pain goes.

After several hospital attendants, doctors, and nurses finished poking, picking, and probing my body, I was bandaged to the point that I resembled a mummy. Then I was forced to spend the duration of the weekend in the hospital.

When I was discharged, we returned to Curtis's parents' home. Bobbie had told my folks that I had been hurt in the motorcycle accident. They came by to see me and were distraught to find me in such a bad condition. My mother recommended that I go to her doctor until I was completely healed and able to return to work. To this day, the thought of getting on a motorcycle or even any one of my family members expressing the desire to ride is forbidden if it is left up to me.

After two years at National Dollar, I was growing tired of working at what seemed to be a dead-end job. So, I decided to look for a position elsewhere. I began responding to want ads in the classified section of several local newspapers. I also registered at the State Employment Office and made cold calls to some companies that featured help-wanted signs in windows or on buildings. I filled out application after application, took test after test, and went on many interviews. When I wasn't successful, I concluded that something was preventing me from getting a better job. Obtaining a job had always been a piece of cake for me in the past. It used to be that I would complete the application, go to the interview, and before I knew it, I was offered the job.

After many disappointments, I finally got a job at K-Mart Department Store, on Western Avenue and Imperial Highway. I found myself back in the same old rut, performing the same tasks that I had at National Dollar. I examined the reasons for the rejections and realized that employers now wanted more than a high school diploma. So I decided that the best thing for me to do was to go back to school to get some additional training.

When I spoke to Curtis about the idea, he was totally against it. I wondered why and discovered after a few discussions that he was very insecure. He feared that I would get an education and a really good job and would not need him anymore. I thought it was ridiculous for him to think that way. After all, he would share in whatever financial gains I earned.

Despite his objections, I was determined to increase my level of education. And so I enrolled in Webster Career College's legal-secretary program. The college would allow me to take classes to prepare for the GED, and it offered grant programs to assist in paying my tuition and transportation. I had to ride three buses to and from school. I didn't mind that inconvenience because I was so excited about this new challenge in my life. I knew that higher education was the key to my future success.

I enrolled Tyree in the same school that Andre attended. Curtis agreed to make sure that the boys got to and from school every day.

While I was at Webster, I met lots of new and interesting people. The teachers took an interest in the students and encouraged them in every way possible. I took advantage of their support. I focused on my studies and worked hard to get the best grades possible. Believe me, it wasn't easy. With two young boys and a meager income, we barely survived.

Webster Career College had been a modeling school before becoming a career college. Some of the instructors from the modeling school continued to teach business etiquette and other courses. These instructors also ran an after-school modeling program. I received a scholarship to be part of it.

Because I was tall and slender, I had been approached many times by modeling agents prior to enrolling in the program at Webster. But Curtis discouraged me from pursuing a modeling career. In fact, the mere thought of me interacting with a male on a one-on-one basis sent him into a rage. But since the school had offered me this opportunity, I wasn't going to let it pass me by this time. I had gotten into a "groove" in my life and was soaking up all the education I could.

I wished that Curtis were just slightly excited and even more than just a little supportive of my efforts. But I knew that the only thing that would make him happy was for me to quit. He would have probably planned a party the same night if I had done so.

I jumped right into modeling. To my surprise, the walks, the turns, and everything else came very easily for me. In fact, my instructors called me a natural. I kept going to the modeling classes until I finished the legal-secretary course. I finished the nine-month course in seven months, with a 4.0 grade point average.

On my graduation day, my parents, my two boys, and several of my friends sat proudly in the audience. I can still remember the keynote speech, even though I don't remember the name of the speaker.

The speaker told a story about a guy he knew from high school who had been popular because of his ability to dance well and to charm the ladies by dancing with a scarf. While dancing, he would wrap the scarf around his partner, fling it in the air, turn, then catch it and do other little gestures. He remained popular throughout high school because of his ability to be entertaining. After completing college, the speaker returned home to visit his family and ran into his classmate, who was wearing the same clothes and doing the same outdated dance with what appeared to be the same scarf. The moral of the story was that the guy was so concerned about clowning his way into popularity that he forgot that education was more important. The same people whom he danced with and performed for had left him behind. And although this guy still received laughs and a little bit of money from handouts for what he did, his classmates prepared themselves to receive a salary. I remembered thinking, *What a wonderful and meaningful speech.* I thought back to the days when I was the class clown and was glad those days were over. The speech gave me even more encouragement to make something better of my life.

When it came time for me to get my diploma, I looked at Andre and Tyree, who sat bright-eyed with anticipation at hearing their mommy's name called. When I heard my name and the applause that followed, I felt so proud to receive that diploma, as well as an honor award. Although I really hadn't expected to see him, I still was disappointed when Curtis didn't show up on my big day. I thought about how opposed he was to my striving so hard to achieve this goal and how hard he tried to tear me down. In the end, not only did I not allow Curtis's hang-ups to discourage me from reaching this great accomplishment, but I could boast that I was one of the best.

ELEVEN

Andre, Tyree, and Shameka

AFTER THE COMPLEX took on new management, our nice, safe, and quiet surroundings changed drastically. One night, we returned home to find that our apartment had been burglarized. Andre's bike and my record collection were among the items stolen. Losing those particular items hurt more than anything else. Andre had ridden his bike only once; it was brand-new. And many of the records in my collection were irreplaceable.

My boys also began to have problems with some of the new kids in the complex. My sons meant everything to me; I was not going to reside in an atmosphere that was uncomfortable for them. I began considering the idea of moving and changing jobs once again. Not only did I want to buy a house in a nice neighborhood, but I also wanted to find a job with medical benefits.

Searching for a house was first on our list. It took approximately three months to locate the house I wanted. It was a two-bedroom house with an enormous den and a great big backyard for the kids. It was located on Mayo Street, in Compton. I had earned enough money for a down payment and got the house financed.

It was located in a very nice neighborhood. The other homes were well kept, and we were surrounded by a wonderful group of neighbors. Andre began attending Roosevelt Junior High School, which was located a few blocks from our house. Tyree continued going to Mark Twain Elementary School near my parents' house.

After we moved into our new home and settled down, I started looking for a better job. I began my job search like a soldier, armed with my diploma, letters of recommendation from the teachers at Webster, and a positive attitude. The search for a job was very short. Because I needed the income, I had to settle for one of the first positions that was offered to me, at Austin-Bradlee.

The company supplied personalized gifts for other companies' employees on their birthdays. We had lots of employees in our files from many companies. We would pull the employees' names during their birthday months, note the gifts that had been selected for them, engrave their names on the gifts, and make sure they received the gifts on their birthdays.

The company was very small. There were only eight employees, including the president. I was one of three general clerks. There was also an engraver, two shipping clerks, and two salespersons. Like a family, we worked and blended well together. Although I enjoyed working there, deep in my heart, I knew that I had not gone to school to end up with a job paying me twenty-five cents more than I had made working for K-Mart.

During my second month on the job, I discovered I was pregnant with my fifth and, what I hoped would be, my last child. I was reluctant to tell my boss that I was expecting since I had been there for only a short while. And I wasn't sure what the company policy was toward pregnant employees.

When I finally got up enough nerve to tell him, I was relieved to find that he was very understanding. In fact, he congratulated me. I was glad that work wasn't a problem, but I was still concerned about the hardship that having another child would present to my home life. I eventually would have to take maternity leave, which would ultimately present financial problems. But my mom always said, "The Lord never put a mouth here that he couldn't feed." With that in mind, I continued to work and decided that I would cross that bridge when the time came.

Andre was very quiet and always kept any problems he had to himself. I had to pay close attention to him to know if he wasn't feeling well or to know if something was bothering him, because he just wouldn't say.

After we had lived on Mayo for a few months, Andre began attending Vanguard Junior High School, the same school that I had attended. His grades started to drop in some of his subjects. I received calls and notes from his teachers about his lack of interest in some of his subjects and about his truancy. A number of times, our neighbors reported seeing Andre sitting on my parents' front porch during school hours. I was very upset, but I knew there must be a reason. Instead of yelling at him, I remained calm so that I could determine the cause.

I began calmly counseling him about the importance of getting good grades in all subjects and about how missing school could be a major problem. He responded well to my approach and began trying to bring his grades up in all his classes. He stopped skipping school, but the problem with his grades continued.

Andre had typically done well in math. But one day, I got a letter from the principal's office, stating that the teacher wanted to meet with me about Andre. When I got there, I just knew that he was in some kind of trouble. As he and I sat in the office waiting for the conference to begin, one of his teachers, Mr. Wright (my former teacher at Mark Twain), rushed into the office and noticed Andre and me sitting there. He said, surprisingly, "Silverson, how are you?" I responded that I was fine. He then looked at Andre and said, "Is he yours?" to which I replied, "Yes." Then, "Now I see why this kid is so sharp." I was relieved to know that I wasn't being summoned to re-solve a problem. Instead, Mr. Wright had called me to say that Andre was too advanced for his current math class, and that he wanted to put him in a special class to learn a higher level of math.

I was relieved to know that Andre's difficulty in school was only due to a lack of interest. He was simply bored and needed more challenge. I consented to the change immediately.

After the problems with Andre's education were resolved, I began to concentrate on the many problems that were occurring in my personal life.

Curtis and I were still party people, although we had calmed down from the way it used to be. It was not uncommon for friends and relatives to drop by anytime, unannounced. A few people would come over, and before you knew it, we had a house full. The guys would all group together in one room, laughing and discussing the world's problems, while the ladies would gather in another room, usually the kitchen, to have their own discussions. Both groups would eventually "dollar up" enough money to buy snacks and drinks. Someone would go pick up what we needed. The kids would have fun playing in the den.

Andre would do what he enjoyed—which was spinning the records. Our friends would sometimes give him a dollar or two for his efforts.

People had begun to form van clubs all over the place. Our group of friends decided we needed to do the same. With the help of my parents, who helped us cash in on an old life insurance policy, Curtis and I purchased our first van. Pretty soon, all the guys in our little circle had purchased vans. We were able to form a club of our own. We held several meetings to discuss the logistics of creating the club. After a short debate, we decided on the name "All for One Van Club." We chose that name because the members of our club were all family and friends—thus, one family.

Whereas before we used to go camping, we now began traveling from one place to another on what were called *van runs*. The van runs were competitive and lots of fun. We would compete against other van clubs in relay races. There were contests for the kids, for the ladies, and for the men. Some of the contests were co-ed. Winners received trophies. Our club took home many trophies.

At the destinations of the van runs, each club would form a circle that resembled the old wagon-train camps. All the clubs were welcome to visit one another's circles. The best part of these outings was that everyone, regardless of race, age, or gender, partied together the entire weekend. There were no incidents. There was nothing but pure unadulterated fun.

On the weekends that we were not on van runs, we spent time raising money for the next one by having house parties. Our family and another family, the Morgans, hosted most of the house parties because our homes had the most space. We sponsored other fund-raising events as well. Some of the more successful ones were the Hot Goblin Jam (a Halloween party) and our San Diego Jazz Festival Run, which took place in the spring every year at Jack Murphy Stadium, in San Diego. Our van club would book rooms at hotels for the entire weekend. These van club events were truly the highlight of my life.

We had a party scheduled for November 20, 1976, at our house. At that time, I was nine months pregnant.

On Sunday afternoon, the week before the house party, Curtis and I were entertaining a member of the van club and his wife when I felt a little pain. I went quickly to the bathroom where I stayed a while. As soon as I returned, I felt another pain and left the room again. No one questioned my frequent trips to the bathroom, maybe because they expected a pregnant woman to go to the bathroom often. After my third or fourth trip to the bathroom, I called Curtis into the room to tell him that I thought it was time to go to the hospital. I wanted him to remain calm. But he ran out of the bathroom, yelling, "It's time! It's time!" Everyone jumped up excitedly, hurrying to get the things I needed for going to the hospital. He loaded the kids and me into the van and began driving rapidly. We must have broken several traffic laws and probably put a few people's lives in danger, including our own. But, thank God, we arrived at the hospital safely and in record time.

After the nurse examined me, I was immediately wheeled to the delivery room. She obviously didn't realize how far along my labor was because she took her sweet time getting there, stopping on occasion to chat with other nurses. Much to her surprise, by the time she started to prep me for delivery, the baby was already coming. She was forced to deliver the baby by herself. Moments later, on Sunday, November 14, 1976, I gave birth to a healthy six-pound, fourteen-ounce baby girl. I named her Shameka Denee Crayon. My doctor finally arrived shortly afterward to finish up the delivery procedures. As the nurse caught her breath, she asked me if I had heard of natural birth. I told her that I had. "Well, that sure is what you had," she said, panting.

I was in the hospital for about three days. Lots of friends and relatives visited me and our new bundle of joy.

When we got back home, many of the van club members came by. They wondered if we should cancel the house party that was scheduled for Saturday. I told them that the party was still on. Our den was located at the rear of the house, away from the bedroom, so I didn't think it would be a problem to go on with the plans. I thought it would be more difficult to relocate the party. The party was a success. It was also the last van club party given at our house on Mayo Street.

Right after Shameka was born, Curtis and I started having problems again. The arguments got so severe at times that I wished we had never gotten back together again. Many of our arguments centered around the fact that Curtis continued to have a relationship with a woman whom he had started seeing while we were separated. I had had a relationship with someone else during our separation that I eventually stopped because I didn't feel comfortable having the relationship around my children. On the other hand, Curtis didn't seem to know how to break off his relationship, so he continued to inconspicuously see her, even after we got back together. He allowed her to call our home, and she would even show up at our van parties. When I finally had had enough of Curtis's disrespecting our home and our relationship, I told him I wanted to break up for good.

Even though the relationship was officially over, the children and I remained in the house on Mayo along with Curtis. Neither of us had the money to move.

Curtis still tried to exercise control over me. He started monitoring the time I spent away from home and sometimes accused me of seeing someone. I guess he recalled the doggish things he had to do to cheat on me. I am sure that his conscience must have beaten the hell out of him to even think about me doing the same.

My supervisor at Austin-Bradlee called to ask when I would be returning to work. They wanted me back as soon as possible and were willing to work around my schedule, considering I had a one-month-old baby. Because Curtis worked from 3:30 P.M. to midnight, I consented to work from 8:30 A.M. until 2:00 P.M. This way, Curtis would be home with Shameka, and I would get home before he left for work. If he needed to leave a few minutes before I got home, Andre and Tyree would handle watching their baby sister.

Although I faithfully worked this schedule, I wasn't able to save very much money in order to move. After an argument with Curtis one weekend, I realized I had to find a better-paying job if I was ever going to get out of the situation. On Monday, I called my supervisor and told him I would be absent for the rest of the week. I spent the entire week job hunting. I applied at Panasonic and McDonnell Douglas Aircraft Company. At McDonnell Douglas, I took an aptitude test and a typing test. I failed the typing test by only a few words. Although I could type sixty words per minute and passing the test only required fifty words per minute, my nerves got the best of me, so I didn't type at my usual speed and accuracy. I was offered a second chance, but I failed once again. The interviewer told me to go home and practice and come back to take the test for the third time the following week.

By that Friday, I had applied for jobs with at least a dozen companies. I was bound and determined to land a better-paying job. I had to do better on the typing test on Monday. As soon as I arrived home that Friday afternoon, the telephone rang. It was a representative from Panasonic, offering me a job. I was prepared to start work on Tuesday at 8:30 A.M.

I spent the entire weekend considering my options. I decided to retake the typing test at McDonnell Douglas because the job there paid more and provided better benefits. Early Monday morning, I went back to McDonnell Douglas to take the test for the final time. My attitude was that if I passed it, I would get the job. If not, I still had the job waiting for me at Panasonic. Luckily, I passed the test. I was given a physical, took the picture for my badge, and was told to report to work on Wednesday.

I began working at the Long Beach location of McDonnell Douglas as an operations control analyst. After I had been employed approximately four months, the company moved me to the Torrance location for part of the day. They would send me from Long Beach at midday to Torrance, where I would do the same job. I was transported back to Long Beach at the end of the day. Then the company determined that it needed me to work all day at the Torrance location. And so I spent the rest of my thirteen-year career with McDonnell Douglas working at that location.

Although I spent a lot of time working, I still found time for my household chores and my children. There were many weekends when I would have a house full of kids. All of my friends knew that I loved children and that I had no problem watching theirs. Andre and Tyree were not allowed to spend the night away from home too often, but I let their friends and relatives spend nights frequently with us.

Both boys had expressed some interest in karate, so I enrolled them in a martial arts school. I took them to classes when I got off work in the evenings. Curtis didn't seem to like the idea of Andre and Tyree attending karate school (maybe he thought someday they might be able to beat him up). So I never really told him that we were going. Each day they would bring their karate uniforms home, wash them, and hide them until the next day. Working full-time and then coming home, getting the baby ready, and taking the boys to karate every day kept us all busy, but we managed.

TWELVE

Warren

AT MCDONNELL DOUGLAS, I met Warren Griffin, one of the few black men working in an upper-management position. We became good friends and spent many lunches and breaks together. We would share personal problems with one another and also had a few good laughs. He was nice and a good person to talk to. We enjoyed each other's company very much. There were a few other employees in our small circle at McDonnell Douglas that shared in the fun with us. It felt great to have a good job and to be surrounded with good and positive people. I felt even more of an incentive to leave Curtis and to develop a new lifestyle for my kids and me. I knew I had to secure a place before I could make my move. And I had to plan my move without Curtis's knowledge as I was sure it would cause an ugly confrontation.

Christmas came and went pretty uneventfully for me. The kids enjoyed themselves as usual. I did not look forward to going to a party at Curtis's brother Donald's house on New Year's Eve. I went with two of my girlfriends, Julia and Donna. We planned to show our faces at the party and then leave. Right after the countdown into the new year, Julia, Donna, and I left the party. We needed to go to one of our homes to sit, talk, and enjoy the rest of the evening away from men because all of us were having man problems. We chose Julia's place.

She was living with Curtis's cousin James. While we were sitting in her bedroom, I suddenly heard the sound of a muffler on a van. Neither Julia nor Donna heard anything. They both claimed that it was my imagination. We continued discussing our relationship problems, and then I heard someone at the door of the bedroom where we were. Once again, I was the only one to hear it because the other women were so busy talking that they only heard each other.

All of a sudden the bedroom door flew open, and there stood James in the doorway. He calmly and politely asked Julia to come out for a minute. A few minutes after she left the room, we heard a loud clapping sound. After that, we heard Julia scream. Donna and I both stood up to go to her defense but thought that doing so would be overstepping our boundaries. Julia never came back in the room. However, James made several trips into the room, never saying a word to us. He was carrying the dresser drawers from the room. When I finally went outside to see what was going on, I saw a pile of Julia's clothes in the front yard. James was taking the drawers and dumping her things there. Julia picked them up and neatly placed them in the trunk of her car.

I attempted to help her, but James asked me nicely to let her do it herself. To avoid further trouble, I obeyed his request and returned to the house. Donna and I decided that after Julia was done packing, I would offer to let her come stay at my house until she could find a place of her own. She was aware of my plans to leave Curtis and understood that her stay would be very short.

I suggested to Julia that she apply for a job at McDonnell Douglas. She did so and was hired right away. This worked out perfectly for both of us. We would ride to and from work together, and after work we would search for apartments and houses to rent.

We found a house for rent in Carson, near Avalon and Victoria Streets. The house was in pretty bad shape, but it was affordable and was located approximately fifteen minutes from our jobs. It was a three-bedroom, two-bathroom house with a large backyard and patio.

Every evening for three weeks, we got off work, picked up Andre and Tyree, and would go to work on the house for a few hours. The boys didn't mind missing karate because they were excited about moving. A few of the guys from work helped us out with the heavy work. This included Warren, whose friendship with me had blossomed into an intimate relationship. He helped with the painting and other tasks.

Julia and I successfully completed the tasks that were necessary to make the house a decent and comfortable place to live— cleaning the carpets; painting the entire house inside and out; adding missing doorknobs, switch plates, and light fixtures; fixing pipes in one bathroom; putting ceramic tile on the bathroom wall and floor; stripping the paint off the kitchen cabinets and staining them; replacing the tile on the kitchen floor; installing the missing sliding glass door in the kitchen; rescreening the patio; and having the junk hauled away from the backyard. People who saw the house in its beginning stages could not believe the finished product. They especially could not believe that two women nearly rebuilt what was a run-down place into a nice house to live in.

After all that work, we only lived in the house for approximately six months. We moved after the owner refused to fix the plumbing problem.

I moved back to my parents' house. Julia moved in with her new friend, Robert. Shortly after the kids and I moved back to my parents' house, Warren started talking about the possibility of the two of us buying a house together. I thought it was a good idea since Warren and I had so much in common and he seemed so interested in my well-being.

Warren and I searched for a house and eventually settled on one located on Thorson Street, in Compton. Before we made the final decision to buy the house, we observed the neighborhood and its surroundings for two weeks in the evenings, mornings, and weekends. We saw one kid the whole time. We were overwhelmed by the quiet, peaceful atmosphere and decided to take the house.

After we moved in, we discovered that the neighborhood was *full* of kids. Kids seemed to have come out of the woodwork. And they all enjoyed hanging out at our house. My children were very friendly and well liked throughout the neighborhood.

Andre was a magnet for kids. He seemed to get along well with everyone. Tyree was also a very friendly person who attracted kids in several age groups. Shameka had her own group of friends as well.

Warren and I decided that we wanted his only son, Warren III, better known as "Little Warren," to live with us. However, his ex-wife would have no part of the plan after she found out that his dad and I were living together. I assumed it was because she didn't want another woman raising her child. Warren had four children altogether—three girls and a boy. He was very fond of his children and spent a lot of time with them.

We began talking about getting married. Although it is said that "the third time is the charm," I wasn't so sure about that. Warren and I had many problems that we needed to iron out. He was a wonderful person with a good heart and good intentions. However, at times, he did extra things for his kids, which presented an overwhelming financial problem for us. There was obvious jealousy on the part of the children's mother. She seemed to use the kids to make problems for us. I tried to be a trooper and continued to do what was needed to maintain our lifestyle. However, it was very difficult for us to take care of our own obligations when so much money was going out of the household to support Warren's kids.

I thought a lot about how much I had invested in the house we had just purchased together. I didn't want it to be another mistake. We had a few debates about how we could try to combat the problems we were having with our children, his children's mother, and the finances. We set guidelines to make each other feel more comfortable about dealing with one another's kids. We also established a budget so that we would feel more financially stable. After things started to flow a little better, we decided to go ahead with the wedding plans.

I wanted a small, simple wedding with just the two of us. He wanted a big wedding with everyone present. I gave into his desire to have a big wedding so long as we could keep the cost low. All of our kids were going to be in the wedding, along with Warren's brother George, my cousin Lois, and a friend named Rose. To keep the cost to a minimum, we did most of the work ourselves. I made my dress and all of the bridesmaids' dresses. We were able to get the invitations at a good deal, and my friends and I cooked the food for the reception. The wedding and the reception came off without a hitch, and we received lots of compliments.

Shortly after we were married, Warren came home from work and told me that McDonnell Douglas plant workers at the location where he worked were planning to go on strike. This was not good news at all. We knew that he needed to work and felt that crossing the picket line was not a good idea. The strike went on for more than a month, causing our finances to suffer. We were behind on all of our bills. When the strike was finally over and Warren had returned to work, his department began laying off workers. We were very worried at that point.

We also had another challenge. Warren had an old knee injury that flared up and gave him excruciating pain at times. He went on medical leave right before he was scheduled to be laid off work. Weeks passed before he received any money from his disability benefits. Fortunately, he was spared from the layoff.

Warren was paying child support and also providing additional money for the kids' necessities that their mother wasn't providing.

Although it wasn't fair that she wasn't living up to her financial responsibilities, he had no choice but to take care of his kids, whom
he loved so much. We could not let them go without the things
they needed because of her. We struggled financially, with seemingly no way of reducing our financial burden. In addition, we had
the added responsibility of his son, Little Warren, who had started
to spend more time in our home, despite his mom's objections.

When Little Warren stayed weekends, he would cry when it
was time to go home. So we started allowing him to stay during
the week. Because it was summer, school was not an issue. Eventually, he stayed with us every day.

When the summer ended, we asked if Little Warren could stay
with us permanently. His mother reluctantly consented and was
probably greatly relieved to have one less mouth to feed.

With children, the end of summer is like the beginning of another year. We had to be concerned about school schedules, school
clothes, lunches, and homework. In my case, it caused me to reflect
on what I had gotten my kids and myself into with Warren's kids
and their mother. His sudden reduction in income made me wonder if my dream of providing a happy life for my kids would ever
come true. I was beginning to feel that I had "jumped out of the
skillet and into the fire" by marrying Warren. The idea of bringing
my kids from one struggle into another made me very unhappy.

Somehow I had to find a way to prevent myself from becoming
a three-time loser in marriage. I constantly assured my children
that everything was going to be all right.

One evening, the mother of Warren's children came to our
house, demanding more money. Warren told her that he was not

giving her any more money, and she whipped out a knife. I asked her to leave my house, but she refused. Shameka and Little Warren were crying hysterically. Tyree was trying to take the kids out of the room before they got hurt. It was a mess. After she said she didn't give a damn about upsetting the kids, I left the room and went to the porch to get an iron. I swung the iron at her, hitting her in the head. She immediately fell to the floor. Fortunately for her and me, I came to my senses and didn't hit her again.

As she headed for the door, I tried to talk to her about her actions. I don't know if what I said was received because we were both so angry. But she did leave the house.

THIRTEEN

Dr. Dre

ANDRE ENTERED CENTENNIAL High School in 1979. I vowed to keep a close watch on his school performance to avoid the problems we had experienced the year before. For a while, he seemed to be doing quite well, as far as going to school every day and maintaining decent grades. He was like most students—he excelled in some subjects and was just average in others.

Andre's favorite class was drafting. His drafting instructor wanted him to enroll in an apprenticeship program at Northrop Aviation Company, but his grades in some of the other subjects were not good enough. Unfortunately, not being able to take advantage of this opportunity seemed to have a negative effect on him and his grades. I became really concerned and figured that a change of scenery might help. I allowed him to transfer to Fremont

High School, in Los Angeles, where Curtis's little brother, Daryl, was attending.

Needless to say, he started having the same problems at Fremont that he had experienced at the other schools. He also began ditching classes. We went through battle after battle about his attendance at school and his grades. As before, he excelled in the classes he liked, but his grades suffered in the classes he didn't like. His swimming instructor begged me to do what I could to help Andre bring his grades up. Andre was his best diver, but he couldn't remain on the swim team unless his grade point average was C or better. His English teacher said, "I know he's not a dummy; I watch him play chess at lunchtime, and he beats everybody." She continued, "Students line up to challenge him, yet he remains undefeated."

I didn't know what else to do. I thought I had done all that I could. I let him go to the school of his choice; I talked with him continuously; I talked to his teachers; I even threatened him. Yet nothing seemed to work.

Andre was also a very handsome young man, which drew the attention of many young girls. During the time when I was raising Andre, I instilled in him, as well as in his sister and brother, the values of neatness, cleanliness, respect, and prosperity. I did talk to him about sex and how to protect himself, and to respect his girlfriend. I know now that I fell a little short on that subject. I should have leaned on the subject of sex a little harder. Maybe man-to-son talks work better than mom-to-son talks when it comes to sex. Men have a way of getting right to the facts and telling it like it is. I think that every father should have those man-to-man talks with their sons. It's not guaranteed to stop them from making mistakes, but it sure as heck will put something in their minds. The men in Andre's life were my second and third husbands. The third one, Warren, did have a conversation with Andre about sex, but it may have been a little late.

During this time Andre met a young lady named Lisa Johnson. Her mother thought it was a little early for Lisa to start dating, so (we all found out later) the couple started ditching school to be with each other. She lived in Culver City and was attending school at Fremont High as well. I had one or two brief telephone conversations with her. Once, she invited Andre and one of his friends over for an Easter celebration at her house. I dropped them off, and her mother brought them back home. I guess I could have met Lisa face-to-face then, but it just didn't seem to be that important at the time.

Not long after that, Lisa called and asked me if she could come to our house to visit Andre. After careful consideration, I agreed. A few minutes later, her mom called to say that Lisa was too young to be courting. I was confused because she had allowed Andre to have Easter dinner with Lisa in their home. We each agreed to talk to our children. We had a somewhat cordial conversation to discuss how the very people you don't want your kids to see are the ones they tend to want to see. Teenagers have a natural need to defy authority, especially when it comes to relationships.

Then, one day, I received *that phone call*—the call that all moms of teenagers dread. Lisa's mom called to inform me that Andre had been sneaking over to their house, and that Lisa was now pregnant. Andre was seventeen and Lisa was sixteen. I didn't even know Andre was still seeing Lisa, much less going to her home to have sexual relations with her. When I asked her if she was sure that it was Andre who had been with Lisa, she got very upset. She said, "If I had come home and caught that nigger in my house, you would have been picking him up in a box."

Needless to say, the conversation went downhill from there. I understood her anger, but she was talking about my son. When someone's making a threat against your child, regardless of the circumstances, that's just not something that you want to hear. I couldn't maintain my composure. I became defensive and told her that if she had harmed my son, there would have been no place that she could hide that I could not have found her.

I finally brought the discussion back to her daughter. "My son didn't break in your house and rape your daughter; she let him in, which makes her just as much at fault as he is," I said.

We finally hung up, both still angry but knowing that we had a baby to think about.

Andre and I again had a long talk, but this time it was about him being a father. He listened for a long time and finally admitted to having sex with Lisa. I told him that I wanted him to do right for the baby, but I didn't suggest he get married, like my parents had suggested to me. After all, he was only seventeen, and Lisa was only sixteen.

Lisa's mother would not let Andre see Lisa anymore.

No one called to tell us when Lisa went into labor, so we were not at the hospital on January 19, 1983, when La Tonya Danielle Young was born.

Andre managed to sneak into the hospital and see his new baby girl a few days later. I bought an assortment of baby items and sent them to Lisa.

After a few months passed, Lisa brought the baby to our house for our family to see. I was thirty-three years old and already a grandmother.

I wondered if I had been too easy on Andre. I wondered whether my relationship problems with men had affected my children. Before we could get the baby problems resolved, Andre turned nineteen and became too old to attend high school. I knew how important a high school diploma was and felt that I had failed my child.

Still, it would not be good for him to just lie around the house. One of my ironclad rules was that if you lived under my roof, you had to be productive. You had to be either going to school or working or both. Well aware of my rule, Andre came home to tell me that he had enrolled himself in Chester Adult School, in Compton. I asked him how he expected to do well in that school if he hadn't done well in regular school. He simply said, "The people who go to this school don't act crazy."

Andre excelled at Chester Adult School. He decided to go on to broadcast school. We had to scrape up the money. I took him to the school for his first day of orientation and spent more than half the day with him. After orientation, he decided that he didn't want to go there after all. He said he felt as though the school was more about getting rich than helping students gain skills. He didn't want to risk my money on something that he didn't have a positive feeling about. Though I was disappointed, I was also thankful to him for making such an unselfish decision. Still, I wanted him to find something positive to do with his life. I refused to let him be idle. I constantly encouraged him to look for a job.

Andre had always managed to hold himself together at home. He had remained calm, cool, and collected, no matter what was going on around him.

One day Andre mentioned to me that he wanted to go and stay with his grandparents. I thought that it was because he had never been comfortable with the way we lived. I thought it may have been because there was so much unfairness surrounding the money coming out of our household. As unfair as it may seem, when you get married, you inherit your mate's problems.

After he left, I kept in constant contact with him, trying to convince him to come back home. I knew he was in good hands at my parents' house, even though my dad would sometimes get a little grouchy.

Andre soon left their house, got in touch with his dad, and went to stay with Theodore. His dad was still a drug dealer, even while Andre was living there.

In fact, Theodore was arrested during this time period. Luckily, Andre was not at home. Theodore's youngest sister, Debra, brought Andre back home and told us what had happened. I hated hearing about Theodore's troubles, but I was glad to have my son back, unharmed. I tried hard to keep peace in my home so that Andre would not leave again.

Soon after moving back home, Andre took up an interest in dance. He and two of his friends, Darrin and "June Bug," started a dance group. At the time, a dance called the Pop Lock was popular. Andre and his dance group competed in many contests, but never finished any higher than second place. He quickly got tired of losing and decided to pick up deejaying, something that he felt he was good at and had enjoyed as a child.

In 1984, Andre asked for a music mixer for Christmas. He wanted to attach it to his music system and two turntables, which would allow him to repeat a chosen part of a record without skipping the beat. Warren and I did all we could to make sure that we enjoyed a wonderful Christmas as a family. We made sure that each one of our seven kids got at least one thing that they asked for out of the many gifts that we bought for them.

Andre was so excited when he unwrapped his mixer. He immediately got dressed and went out to show some of his friends before setting it up. He remained in his room all day, practicing with his mixer. I had to beg him to take a break just to eat.

That night after all of the guests had left and the other kids had all gone to sleep, I went into Andre's room to check on him. He was lying on his bed fast asleep, with his headset still on his head and the music blasting. I took the headset off, turned off the music, and threw a blanket over him, trying hard not to disturb his sleep. From that day forward, Andre took his place as the music person of our household.

At times, some of the neighbors would complain about the loud music. I would tell them that I was glad to hear the music because I always knew where my children were. I reminded them that they were not breaking into houses or disabling people by selling them drugs. My reasoning was, "If you take my children's music away from them, what will they have to do?"

My house became party central. Just about every kid on the block would come by at some point during the day. This was a good thing as far as I was concerned. Their parents knew where to find them, and the kids respected my family and me.

The neighbors were right about one thing—the music was really loud. Sometimes I would walk through my house, yelling at the top of my lungs just so I could be heard over the music. Knowing that my kids were home safe made the noise bearable. *It was a fair trade,* I thought.

Andre and a few of his friends formed a deejay group called the Freak Patrol. They would deejay at dances in a park around the corner from our house, as well as at club dances and house parties. Occasionally, I would take Andre, Tyree, and their friends to a club called Eve after Dark, which was a teen club that allowed the kids to showcase their talent on weekends. I would pile as many kids as I could fit into my car (of course, this was before the seatbelt law went into effect) and would drive them to the club at about nine o'clock. I would return home and set my alarm clock for one o'clock in the morning, when I would return to the club to pick them up.

Andre hoped that going to the club would give him the opportunity to showcase his deejaying skills. One night, he was given the opportunity to do so when his godmother's brother, Tim, convinced the club owner to let him show his skills with the turntables. I wish I could have been there to support him, but the club was for young adults. I never dreamed that that one chance to showcase his talent would mark the beginning of a musical legacy.

When Andre got home, he was excited as he told me that he had deejayed, and that the crowd loved it. That club gave Andre his first big break in what would be a very successful career, though I didn't know that at the time. I was simply pleased that he had found something that held his attention and kept him out of trouble.

Shortly thereafter, Andre began calling himself "Dr. Dre, the Master of Mixology." He came up with the "Dr." part from his basketball idol, Dr. J.

A few weeks after his debut as a deejay, as Andre walked near his grandparents' house, the manager of Eve after Dark, Lonzo, approached him and asked if he was the man people called Dr. Dre. When Andre said yes, Lonzo offered him a job as the club's deejay, earning fifty dollars per night.

Andre accepted the job offer and prepared to start immediately. When he told me about his new job, I was as thrilled as he was. I had once told Andre that a job wasn't going to walk up to him and say hello. I smiled as I shook my head because he made me eat my words.

Before long, Andre realized he needed more than fifty dollars a night to make him feel comfortable. During the day, he would hang out at the club with Lonzo and a few of their friends. Andre noticed some recording equipment while hanging out at the club and suggested that they try to do some recording. Although Lonzo thought it was a wild idea, he agreed to it. The idea eventually proved to be a pretty good one.

Andre and his friends put together a group called the World Class Wreckin' Cru. This group consisted of Dr. Dre, Lonzo, D. J. Yella (Antoine), Clientele, and Mona Lisa. The girl, Mona Lisa, was with them for only a short period. She was replaced by Michel'le. Their first record was titled *Turn Off the Lights*. Even though

Andre and the group were selling records, he always seemed to be broke. I couldn't understand why he was constantly asking for loans. Later I found out that the group's manager had purchased a house and a new car, while Andre and the rest of the group were pulling out their pocket linings. Apparently, the money was not filtering down to all of the group's members. I convinced Andre and Antoine to stay with the group, save their money, and get out on their own. Even though I was reluctant about the way business was being handled, I didn't want Andre to give up on the dream he had worked so hard at.

After having a few disagreements with the management of World Class Wreckin' Cru, Andre and Antoine left the group. Andre had no money, but continued to have that same strong determination.

Now that Andre was not with World Class Wreckin' Cru, he knew he would have to start all over again if he was to follow his dream.

One day Andre came home talking about a kid named Eric, who lived a few blocks from us, on Muriel Street. Andre spoke of Eric in glowing terms, often bragging about the nice material things he had. When I asked Andre where Eric worked, he told me that he did not work. Because I had had my share of experiences with men who engaged in illegal activity, I immediately became suspicious of Andre's new friend. I was worried more than anything that Andre would be drawn to the glitter of what drug money could buy. I often told him, "Fast money is not good money." I warned him about the kinds of people it brings and the discomfort it causes from having to look over your shoulder and constantly watch your back. I explained that it was better to live with legal income that trickles in slowly than to deal with the madness that fast money brings, including the possibility of being killed or having his freedom taken away.

Instead of joining Eric in his illegal profession, Andre talked him into combining forces to create a rap group. At first, I think Eric was a little reluctant about the idea, but Andre eventually convinced him to use his money to create a legal business. Andre (Dr. Dre), Eric (Easy E), along with Andre's long-term friend from World Class Wreckin' Cru, Antoine (D. J. Yella) came together. In addition, two other gentlemen who went by the names M. C. Ren (Lorenzo) and Ice Cube (O'Shay, who later joined the group) also joined forces to start a group called N.W.A. (Niggaz with Attitudes). When I first heard the group's name mentioned, I thought, "Oh, my God, what are these fellas thinking?" Hearing the lyrics in their songs sent me into an even greater shock. I never dreamed that this group would advance themselves so quickly to the top of the music charts, and open up the doors for what was called gangsta rap. N.W.A. was known as a controversial group, especially when they came out with the song "Fuck tha Police." I thought I was going to be like Fred Sanford and experience the big one from worrying. After hearing reviews about the song, and the negative things that were said about it, the worry got more and more intense. To my surprise a senator spoke in their defense, and shortly after that Easy was invited to the White House for lunch as a pardon. I had never heard so much talk about a group before. Some would say their lyrics promoted violence. Some had a problem with them referring to women as bitches. The constant complaints made me take a good look at the situation. I started listening to the lyrics, whereas before I had been too busy trying to tune out the profanity, missing the message that was coming across. I also watched the videos, which played a big part in helping me to see beyond the group's name, the lyrics, and the hostility.

It made me remember a time when my boys were standing outside by my car, having a friendly conversation with other boys in the neighborhood, when all of a sudden I looked out the window and saw the police with all of them spread-eagle against the police car. This harassment was for no obvious reason except they saw black boys grouped together and automatically presumed they were up to no good. It was then that I realized that the lyrics in the songs were just stories about things that were actually happening in their lives. Some people just had a hard time getting past the profanity to hear it. The videos also helped me to understand the type of women they described in the songs, who were referred to as bitches. I knew that they were not referring to all women as bitches, only the ones that act a certain way and fit that description. The hostility came from being tired of going through the drill.

The group had a gentleman by the name of Jerry Heller as manager. For the first time in his musical career, Andre was really making progress. From my point of view he was finally receiving his due.

Now that Andre was becoming successful in the music business, our lives were about to be totally reconstructed. Suddenly, we were beginning to see many television and radio interviews highlighting Andre and the new group, N.W.A. Oh, what excitement came over our family to see and hear Andre being interviewed by the media! There was an overwhelming thrill to see him perform on TV, or to hear his voice and his awesome beats on the radio. It was amazing to ride down the street and hear his music blaring from automobiles everywhere we went. Suddenly, the reality of my son's success set in, and I was aware that he had made it. He was the star that he had strived so hard to be. What I thought was most amazing was to see white people of all ages enjoying his music as well.

Our telephone started ringing off the hook. Relatives and friends were calling to announce that they too had read, seen, and heard about Andre in the media. The excitement was everywhere, and all of us were so proud of Andre's great accomplishment.

The first video, "We Want Easy," stands out so fresh in my mind. Easy E, D. J. Yella, Ren, and, of course, Dr. Dre were the awesome four that made up the group N.W.A. They appeared on stage in the video, delivering their message to a beat that had the heads bobbing of everyone in the crowd. One thing about this video that stood out to me was Andre's brother, Tyree, standing in the front row. As the camera focused on Tyree, he stood there, bobbing his head, never missing a beat, sporting a Compton baseball cap. Tyree was Andre's biggest supporter in the whole family. You could rest assured that wherever Andre would appear, Tyree was going to be right there.

Soon, Andre became a father again. And again. Within a few years he had a total of four beautiful daughters. Their names are La Tanya, Tyra, La Toya, and Ashley Young. I was thirty-three years old when my first grandchild was born. Who would have thought that having grandchildren would present me with problems? I guess this is to be expected when there's more than one mother involved.

One mother was very pretty, intelligent, and witty, with personality to spare. The other may have possessed some positive qualities, but I never saw them. She was always involved in a devious scheme to make me miserable, and therefore, I never had the opportunity to see her good side. She would place hang-up phone calls all day to my home as well as to my job; have her men friends call my house, harassing whomever answered my phone with threats; and at times would fabricate stories to get Andre to respond to her. I wondered if she felt that I was somehow responsible for her problems with Andre. After going through this craziness for so long, I came to the conclusion that pestering me was her way of getting through to Andre. She figured that I would complain to Andre, and even though his response would be angry, she would have succeeded in getting his attention.

I tried to keep in close touch with my granddaughters, but eventually got tired of changing phone numbers and going through the crazy stuff, and ended up blocking all communication with them.

One Christmas Eve, I came home from shopping to find La Tonya, La Toya, and Ashley sitting on my steps with Lil' Warren. I asked where their mother was, and Lil' Warren told me that she dropped them off and left saying she would be back shortly. I had them for a few days. I worried because they all had bad colds, and I didn't know if they had any allergies or anything else much about them. They didn't have any extra clothes, so I had to keep washing the clothes they had been wearing. Luckily, I had a few days left from the Christmas vacation that I had been enjoying. As my time off began to dwindle, I worried about what I was going to do with the grandchildren. I started calling the other grandmother to try to track the kids' mother down. I was unsuccessful in finding the mother, but the grandmother finally told me to bring the kids to her. I never knew the reasons for the kids being dropped off that way, but I learned not to be surprised at anything that their mother did.

I tried to love my granddaughters, and to spend time picking them up, letting them spend time with me, but there would always be a problem. This went on for many years, but I learned to put on a tough skin, and ignored a lot of it. I didn't bother Andre with the details. Most of the time he didn't know what was going on. Looking back, I realize that I should have told him what I was going through. By not doing so, I made it easy for the different mothers to tell stories that were in their favor.

It never occurred to me that there was a possibility that Andre would take someone else's word over mine.

FOURTEEN

Heartbreak

I AM NOT SURE when the Crips and Bloods, two rival gangs, became a negative fixture in the schools, but when it came to school shopping, I would take care not to buy anything red or blue, the colors worn by the two gangs.

Tyree was small so he got picked on a lot, but he would never back down from a confrontation. Andre would talk to his brother all the time about fighting, encouraging him to just walk away.

Although I didn't buy red clothing for the boys, Tyree insisted that no one would dictate what he wore. He got a pair of red khaki pants. Since this was the beginning of the gangs' red and blue color wars, those pants eventually got him into trouble.

One evening, I was doing some cleaning when I heard Tyree at a distance, frantically yelling out to me. I ran to the door and saw him running up the driveway, wearing those red pants, and a group of boys was chasing him. I opened the screen door and Tyree slid into the house as if he were sliding into home plate at a baseball game. I immediately grabbed the brass umbrella stand that was by the door and started swinging it. They immediately backed off and ran away. Later that evening, I went into Tyree's room, found those red pants, and threw them in the trash. He never knew what happened to them.

Tyree went through all his years of junior high school having the challenges of people wanting to fight him. During the summer break between junior high and high school, we moved from Compton to North Long Beach. When Tyree transferred from the Compton School District to David Starr Jordan in the Long Beach District, there was a major change in his life. Suddenly, there were no more fights, no constant visits to the school for me, and the worries diminished. Tyree was my athletic child, and participated in high school basketball, football, and track. It was a brand-new day.

With our financial status back on track, Tyree settled in a new school, Shameka doing well at her studies, and Andre making music, I was able to relax. One night I went to a fashion show because my niece Renee was in it. Afterward, I told Renee's mother, Elaine (sister of my ex-husband Curtis), that I could have done the show better. Elaine encouraged me to use the modeling training that I'd received at Webster Career College by putting together a modeling troupe of my own. We ended up creating a group called Distinction Unlimited. The curriculum was based on strengthening self-esteem through training in etiquette, modeling skills, and

[142]

job readiness. The group consisted of children and young adults from the ages of seven to twenty. We had members from all over the city plus my own nieces, nephews, cousins, and other children.

In the beginning stages, Andre was always there to help with the music for the shows. Tyree was one of our star models, and Shameka was always an eager participant.

The day Tyree graduated from high school in June 1986 was extra special to me. I was not only proud that Tyree had made it through high school and had plans to go to college but also proud that he was the first person in our family to graduate from high school. He earned scholarships to go to a few universities, but decided that, rather than going off to college far from home, it would be more economical to enroll in a junior college. Even though I tried to talk him into going to one of the universities, he felt that he should go to junior college until he knew exactly what his major would be so there would be no money wasted.

Tyree was dating a girl named Connie who was having problems at home. So he decided to move to an apartment to live with Connie. I often thought her problems at home stemmed from the fact that Connie was white and her mother didn't approve of her dating a young man who was black. The apartment was only a few minutes away.

Prior to Tyree's relationship with Connie he dated a young lady named Darlene. She moved away and Tyree started dating Connie. During this time, Darlene moved back to the area. Tyree found out Darlene was pregnant. Even though he was living with Connie, he was trying to do right by Darlene, who was pregnant with his child.

He enrolled first at El Camino College and then switched to Long Beach City College. At the same time, he landed a job at Northrop Corporation, an aerospace company located in Hawthorne, California. Shortly after starting work at Northrop, Tyree told me that he and Darleen were going to have a baby. I knew then why Tyree was so enthusiastic about staying close to home.

Tyree and Darlene had a baby boy on September 3, 1987. She named the baby Cedric Jordan Turner. We all questioned her reasons for giving the baby her last name as opposed to giving him Tyree's last name. She told me that she and Tyree were having problems.

Darlene's mother called me one night very intoxicated. She told me that she did not want Tyree with Darlene. Her reasons were not clear. Then she went into a screaming rage. I don't know why she was so mean to Tyree. He was always nice to her daughter, and he simply adored Cedric.

Shortly after our conversation, Darlene's mother moved and took Darlene and Cedric to Oakland, California. Every Friday Tyree would get off work, pack a few things, and head to Oakland to see Cedric.

Tragedy struck on June 4, 1989, when my ex-husband Curtis died of a heart attack. Tyree and Shameka had lost their father. Tyree was so distraught at the funeral that it really caused me to pay close attention to him for days afterward. I don't think he ever fully recovered from the shock. In addition to that, I think that he was beating himself up because he had said negative things about Curtis's absence in his life shortly before his death.

In a short period of time the group N.W.A. became more and more popular, and the time that Andre spent with his family became less frequent. We would fill the void of not having him visit us by going wherever he was. I would sometimes go to the studio, where I would find him sitting in front of a large keyboard with so many knobs and switches that I thought it was amazing how he knew which switch controlled what. I later found out that production would stop while I was there. Out of respect for me, he would not play the music containing bad language (lyrics that N.W.A. was noted for) in my presence. I learned this through a conversation with one of Andre's friends. He said, "Andre has the utmost respect for you. He talks about you all the time. You notice that when you walk in the studio everything stops?" I was surprised to hear that.

Not wanting to stop the group's production, I immediately stopped coming to the studio. I later took the opportunity to tell Andre how proud I was of him and went on to say that I tune out the bad words and listen to the message along with his beats. I think I gained his confidence by letting him know that I had no problem with his music, and we were okay from that point on. I went to his concerts, talk show appearances, parties, and award shows. Andre's success with N.W.A. spread like wildfire. In June 1989, the group went on a multistate tour.

Tyree stopped by for one of his usual visits. I could tell that something was troubling him. When I asked what was wrong, he said, "Everywhere I go, it seems that someone always wants to challenge me to a fight." I sat talking to him, encouraging him, and told him that everything was going to be all right. As I walked him to his car, I told him, "I worry about you, Tyree. Take care of yourself, and please watch your back." At that very moment, a guy turned the corner, and slowed down just long enough to give Tyree the evil eye as he drove by. Tyree was frustrated. "You see! That man doesn't even know me, and he wants a piece of me, too." I told Tyree to come back by later that evening so we could talk some more. I fell asleep waiting for him, but he didn't come back.

The next day I was scheduled to model in Johnnie Jordan's fashion show. I had met him during the time that I was promoting my modeling group, and we supported one another. That morning I woke up with Tyree on my mind. I picked up the phone and called him, but there was no answer. I was feeling halfway between sad and worried. I managed to spark up enough energy to pack my bags and headed off to the show.

Between each scene I would go to the phone booth to call Tyree, hoping with each ring I would hear his voice. After each call, I would try my best to hide my worry and make a good presentation of the clothes I was showcasing.

After the show was over, I rushed home just long enough to put down my bags, make another failed attempt to call Tyree, change clothes, and jump in the car to head to my parents' house. In addition to worrying about Tyree, my dad was also on my mind. He had an illness that affected his equilibrium, and he would fall down without warning. What started about six years prior as an occasional fall had gotten progressively worse. At that point, he was no longer able to walk.

On the way to my parents' house, thoughts of Daddy and his condition along with Tyree and his problems kept replaying in my mind. When I arrived at my parents' house, I went to the bedroom to check on my dad. I then sat in the kitchen with my mother and talked to her about the conversation I had had with Tyree. I broke down crying and told her how worried I was about him. I sobbed and said that maybe a vacation for him, away from all the evils in California, would be a good idea.

That night I tossed and turned. I must have called his apartment at least two dozen times before I finally dozed off.

At 2:30 A.M. I was awakened by Little Warren's knock at my bedroom door. He said that there were two men in my living room who wanted to speak to me because something had happened to Tyree.

I raced to the door. Tyree's best friend, Jerry, stood there, motionless. Two white men wearing suits and carrying briefcases stood on the other side of the room. My heart was racing, but I managed to ask, "What happened to Tyree?"

There was no answer.

I then asked, "Where is Tyree?"

One of the men told me that Tyree had been involved in a confrontation with a gang member, his head had hit the concrete, and he had never regained consciousness.

At that point I started screaming and running. When I came back to myself, I was three blocks from my house, and Big Warren was assisting me back to the house. I couldn't imagine my son dead.

After I calmed down from the initial shock of Tyree's death, I started calling different family members and close friends to tell them the tragic news. Most of them were shocked and confused.

The news spread like wildfire, and our phone began ringing off the hook. Due to the fact that his father had passed exactly three weeks prior to his death, people were confusing the news with thoughts and hopes that they were hearing a replay of Curtis's death.

Andre was still away on a tour with N.W.A. We tried several times to contact him on his cell phone with a 911 emergency signal, but the calls failed. We found out later that because he was going through mountains at the time, the messages came out scrambled.

When Andre finally got to a truck stop and had the opportunity to call home, he was devastated by the news.

His girlfriend at the time, LaVetta, later told us that Andre just fell to his knees and started crying. When she found out what was wrong, she wept, too. She said that everyone got quiet as they all felt his pain. He cut the tour short to come home and be with the family. Andre stuck by me throughout the planning stages of Tyree's funeral. He was very attentive and concerned about my feelings. At the same time, I think we all were trying to be strong for one another.

We received many sympathy cards, phone calls, and visits. The day of the funeral, I thought that everyone in the world who knew Tyree attended the funeral.

After getting through the funeral, it was very hard to adjust to my loss. My precious baby was gone from me. Losing a child is about the worst hurt anyone can ever feel. Holidays were the worst. It was like a link in a chain had been removed. Nothing seemed right anymore. For a while the family drew much closer together. We seemed to cling to one another as if we were attempting to absorb each other's pain.

I couldn't cope. Day-to-day problems that once could have been easily solved or pushed to the back burner simply immobilized me. I knew that I needed help but didn't feel that a mental

Andre and Michel'le (center), Eric "Eazy-E" (right), with backup singers.

Tyree's son, Cedric,
Christmas 1995.

Top: Santa and Marquita,
(Warren Sr.'s granddaughter).
La Tanya, Tyra, La Toya,
Ashley and Shameka,
Andre's daughters and sister.

Tyra Young (Andre's daughter) struttin' her stuff in the last show in honor of Tyree, who passed away during the planning of the show.

La Tanya, Ashley and La Toya Young (Andre's daughters).

Marcel DeAndre Young
(Andre and Michel'le's son),
October 1993, two years
and eight months old. He is
the spitting image of Andre
when he was that age.

Marcel Young.

Warren G and Shameka.

Dena Vernardo (Snoop
Dogg's aunt), Verna's
friend Rosa, and Verna.
They all design fashions.

Verna modeling one of
her designs in a fashion
show held in her den.

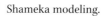
Shameka modeling.

Shameka ready for her
prom (age seventeen).

Warren G modeling in
Verna's modeling group.

Andre's daughter Tyra,
Christmas 1995.

Andre at a family
reunion, 1992.

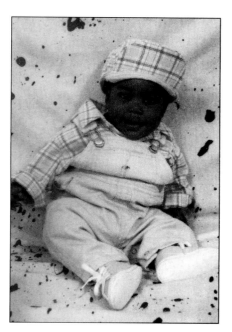

Kion Tyree Williams,
six months old.

Andre and Verna at a video
shoot ("California Love").

Verna and Andre "boogieing down."

Andre and Nicole at a New Year's party.

Verna in Waikiki.

health professional would do any good. My attitude was that they didn't know me and surely had their own problems to solve. It was only when everyone started talking about how bad I looked that I realized how close I was to a nervous breakdown. It was time to get professional help. I did go for counseling sessions that helped me in a big way.

Before Tyree died, he and Darlene had decided that she would join the service. The plan had been for Cedric to live with Tyree during her term. She decided to carry out the plan and enlisted in the United States Navy. One of the requirements for her enlistment was to get someone to take guardianship over Cedric. I volunteered to take care of the legal matter and keep Cedric with me until Darlene finished her necessary training.

Cedric was only a year and a half old when Tyree passed and two years old when I took guardianship. It was a joy to have Cedric with me and to do some of things that I imagined Tyree would have wanted to do for him. As soon as Darlene's boot-camp training was over, she came for Cedric. I was sad to see him go, even though it gave me a time-out. Each time Darlene would get ready to go out to sea, she would bring Cedric back to stay with me. I appreciated the fact that she continued to keep Cedric close to us while he was growing up.

Thanks to the three friends who were with Tyree when he died, justice was served to Tyree's killer.

FIFTEEN

Climbing Back Up

BY THIS TIME, I had worked thirteen years at McDonnell Douglas Aircraft Company. Throughout those years, I witnessed people coming and going. Some of them retired, some died, and some left the company for various other reasons. Then came the "RIF" (reduction in force), which meant there would be many that would fall prey to a vast layoff. The purpose of the RIF was to cut back to adjust the budget, so a lot of the top-paid employees were the first ones to go.

I had always dreamed of owning my own clothing boutique, and in the years prior had put together a plan. I discussed my idea with Andre, and he thought it was good. After searching and comparing shopping centers, malls, and small buildings, Andre and I discussed my options and decided that the Carson Mall would be the best choice. I painted the store white and ordered white wall racks and a white checkout counter trimmed in gold. For the carpet, I chose emerald green.

Because my spot was so large, I hired a friend who was very good at construction to build a wall that would divide the unused space from the boutique. He also added a nice-sized platform/stage with an extra large cathedral-shaped mirror and dressing rooms. The stage was to serve two purposes: an area for the customers to walk, turn, and get a better view of the garments in the mirror; and occasionally it would be a runway for in-store fashion shows. I completed the decor with a few round clothing racks, a couple of plants, and a white rattan settee for significant others to sit on while their ladies shopped.

After being in business for approximately two months, I had the grand opening. Michel'le came to the store to make an appearance and to sign autographs. Many people showed up to meet her—the little lady with the cutest squeaky speaking voice who possessed the most powerful delivery when she sang. She was amazing. I really appreciated her for coming out and supporting me that way.

Being a store owner was a lot of work, and the hours were long. There were days when the sales were good, but more days when there was very little income. The best days were when I held fashion shows in the store or other special occasions. The shows were advertisements and sales tactics that worked, but fashion shows were not enough to keep the store profitable. The mall traffic was not very good, and I found out that black people (my people) were the worst when it came to patronizing. White people would come in my store, make a selection, and usually pay with a credit card, not being concerned with the price. Hispanic people would critique the garment, look at the price tag, discuss it in their language, and then bring it to the counter and pay with cash. Black people would critique the garment and the price tag, and then ask, "What can you give this to me for?" It was as if they were doing me a favor by coming in my store, and I owed them something for that. I knew my prices were comparable, or better than, the prices in the major shops in the mall. I had researched to make sure my prices were the best for the designer fashions I carried before opening.

I would also get heckled by black women passing by. They would say things like, "She thinks she's something." "Who does she think she is bringing something like this to the Carson Mall?" I had my first example of the "crabs in the barrel" syndrome that I had heard described so many times in my life. Even though I was faced with a lot of discouragement, I continued to keep the faith that the store would prosper.

The mall's hours were from 10:00 A.M. to 9:00 P.M. weekdays, and it was also open on weekends and holidays. Some of the passersby would come in and spend hours looking at the fashions and talking with me. There were people that would actually stop in and tell me their life story. I received so many visits of this type that I thought it might be a plus to put up a sign that read "Help Center." After I had given the business venture my all, profits were still not enough to afford the store's bills.

I gave the business a lot of thought, mainly ideas on how I could make the store work. I thought about purchasing or leasing sewing machines, hiring seamstress, and manufacturing my own fashions to sell and eliminate the middleman. This idea would bring bigger profits for the store. There were a few drawbacks to the idea: my funds were running low; I didn't know how to make patterns; and I didn't have enough knowledge of the fashion industry to risk jumping into something so challenging; the money I had was not enough to hold out through the time it would take to get the fashion production up and running.

I was stuck in the middle of a very hard decision, with too much to lose, yet not enough to continue, and still not willing to give up. One day while sitting idly in the boutique, I made a couple of ensembles that included a hat, a shawl, and shoes covered in matching African fabric. I found that as fast as I made the ensembles, they sold. Customers were amazed that I could cover shoes. I was doing well for a while, then suddenly the sales on the ensembles stopped. It was then that I realized that people bought the ensembles as costumes only to be worn during Black History Month. It was hard for me to understand why "my people" identified with their heritage only during February, the shortest month of the year. The fabrics were beautiful, and there was a certain amount of pride in every woven thread. As the months went by, I grew weary of the situation. I finally came to the conclusion that the store was not profitable, and there was no way that I could turn it around with the little money I had left.

One day, a lady wandered into the store and identified herself as Nadine Petre, a fashion designer. At that moment, I thought maybe this would be the opportunity to get the design idea started. We talked briefly about her skills as a designer, her background in producing patterns, her experience in the clothing manufacturing business, and how she could help me reach my goal. She left and later returned with a portfolio of her own sketches and a résumé that included a few years of experience with several clothing manufacturing companies. That evening I went home and pondered the idea of closing the store and using the remainder of my money to create a line of clothing to sell to stores. I thought about how this would eliminate the long hours I had spent making money only for the mall, and dealing with so many negative people. I just knew that if given an opportunity, I could make something work to put me back in a stable financial category that would enable me to take care of my family.

I started gathering information by reading and asking my designer friends a lot of questions about the fashion industry. I also read to refresh my memory on the subjects of record keeping and small business management. Shortly after cramming for information on the aspects of the clothing business, I called Nadine and set up a meeting to discuss the fashion business venture.

Upon meeting with Nadine, we made an agreement that she would supply the direction and work skills, while I was to supply the money and labor to get the clothing line started. I also discussed the approximate dollar amount that it would take to create and market the line. This was important to me, because I didn't want to jump into something that I could not afford. The figure she gave me was acceptable. We got off to a good start, sketching fashion ideas, selecting fabrics and trims, and setting up a work space suitable to complete the venture.

What started out as an exciting and promising business venture quickly turned dismal. Most of the samples sewn from the patterns Nadine made had drastic mistakes, and she started spending a lot of time working on her own line instead of following through with our agreement. I didn't mind her having an interest in her own line, but I felt that she should have waited until my line was finished and doing well so that we would have funds for her line as a subdivision. The final analysis was that she was using me to get a line started that she didn't have funds for. I overheard her talking to someone on the phone one day saying, "I've been so busy doing everything around here, and Verna, she don't know nothing." I was surprised and disappointed with her remark. After all, I had worked just as hard or harder to make this work.

I finally decided to quit when I couldn't count on Nadine coming in every day. I cleared my things out of the shop and took them home to be stored in my garage and my sewing room. Nadine called, offering excuses for her absence, but I simply told her that I felt the business was going nowhere. Even though I knew the reason for the business's demise was that she didn't carry out her part of the agreement, I listened to her tell me that she had discussed with her friend that it was my fault the business had failed. At the time, I didn't care one way or the other. The simple fact was that it didn't work, and I was out of it. After hearing her excuses on more than one occasion, I told her that it wasn't my fault—it was her fault. She did finally take partial blame. Again, it didn't matter to me. I just wanted her to know that she couldn't play with my mind. This venture reminded me of a verse of a poem my mom would sometimes quote from a book of "Tyler" poems. She said, "If you ever go into business, don't go out on a limb, 'cause some people will let you drop just to see if you can swim."

It was clear that I needed a job. It turned out that being an ex-employee of McDonnell Douglas was a strike against me. Either my ending salary was too high or my skills did not click with a company's needs. I finally went to an employment agency, and they found me a position at a bank as a file clerk. Neither the work nor the pay was what I was accustomed to, but I always thought that a poor job was better than no job. At least the money would help with bills and the care of my daughter, since my marriage was on the rocks. Warren and I had been having problems that seemed to add to the stress I was already feeling over the loss of both my son and my job.

As Andre's success added up to bigger dollars, I was elated to witness him moving on up in the music industry, growing wiser, and handling his wealth. The day when he went out to see the first house he purchased, he invited me to go with him. We drove to the city of Agoura Hills, a city, until that time, I never knew existed. The city was so nice and clean, and the air seemed so fresh. The house was also nice. I thought it was the nicest home that one could ever dream of. I felt so proud of my son. I was so full of joy, it felt like I was on the brink of suffocating from it. It was like Christmas in the summertime, and I was just as excited as he was. I thought I would burst with pride at the sight of such a beautiful home.

When Shameka and I went to visit Andre, it was like taking a trip. It was a long distance from our house to his, yet we would always be excited to go there to hang out with him. The house had four bedrooms and three baths, and as far as I was concerned it was the most wonderful house I had ever seen. The neighborhood was quiet, and the area was quaint. Both Easy E and the D.O.C. lived in the area, only minutes from Andre's house. Andre had a crew of wonderful friends who were all talented in some capacity. It was so nice to see so many youngsters with the talent and determination to make it. Andre seemed to draw talent. This was good, because when you're talented and making lots of money, you should surround yourself with positive people. The problem is that you have got to make sure that the people aren't hiding behind false faces. You have to know who your true friends are, and who is just there seeking a place to fit in so that they can see what they can get.

Meanwhile, I had received unexpected money from Tyree's job. A representative from the human resource office at Northrop called to let me know that Tyree had come into the office and asked for an extended insurance policy just a few weeks before his death. She told me that she thought it was very unusual for such a young man to think about an insurance policy rather than a car or some other luxury. I followed Andre's advice to do something with the money that I could remember Tyree by, even though he could never be forgotten.

I found a very nice house in Placentia, California, about thirty miles from where I previously lived, and used the money as a down payment. This was the nicest house I had ever had, and in a very nice, quiet, and friendly neighborhood. Things were starting to look up for me, and I owed it all to my children.

Andre had moved on, and Little Warren went to live with his mother. Now there was only Shameka left at home. When Shameka graduated from junior high school, Andre took time out to come to graduation. After the graduation ceremony, Andre was bombarded by students as well as a few parents, signing autographs for almost an hour. Some of the kids had him sign their yearbooks; some had him sign their programs. There were kids that were actually getting paper from the trash cans just to have Dr. Dre's autograph. Every time he thought he was signing the last autograph, more and more kids would come. I finally had to interrupt by telling them, "No more."

Even though we had moved to Placentia, Shameka decided to continue going to school in Long Beach, where all of her friends would be attending David Starr Jordan High School. I would take her to one of her friend's house on my way to work. Her friend lived near the school, and they would walk to and from school together. In the evening, I would pick her up on my way from work. Andre saw how hard it was for me to transport his sister to and from school, so he bought Shameka her first car.

When Shameka graduated from high school, the graduation was held on the football field. Andre and his entourage showed up for her graduation. As they walked onto the field, the people who recognized him stood up and applauded. I stood proudly beside him and thought, *Wow, what a wonderful welcome.* I could see that it made him feel special.

For some reason the school did not prepare for a Grad Night, as it had always done in the past. So I decided to give Shameka a graduation party at our home in Placentia, California. There were so many people at the party. Many of them we had not seen in years, and they showed up in disbelief that Shameka had grown up so fast. Andre had his crew hang out in the front and search people as they came in to make sure there would be no incidents to spoil Shameka's party.

After a year in Agoura, Andre moved to a bigger house. It was fabulous: five bedrooms, five baths, high ceilings. Wow!

One day Andre told me they were going to be shooting a video for the D.O.C. in the city of South Gate at one of the old factory buildings. The shoot was scheduled for the entire weekend. I dropped by on that Saturday evening just about the time they were breaking for a new scene setup. I observed the guys doing a little drinking and warned them that the fog was setting in and it would be hard to see clearly if they were drunk. I told them if they felt themselves getting drowsy it was best to stop off at a hotel, motel, or somewhere.

The following Monday morning, Andre called to tell me that the D.O.C. had been in a horrible accident. My heart sank when Andre described his condition. Thankfully, his life was spared. Then we found out that his voice was altered. It was the craziest thing. I was told that the car was so crushed that it seemed impossible that anyone had survived. Yet he had no broken bones, only a few bad cuts and a few scratches. But the accident had affected his voice. Just as his career as one of the most promising rappers was beginning, it suddenly came to an end.

Although the D.O.C.'s voice was very raspy, I encouraged him to not give up. I thought with prayer and his will to succeed, his voice might come back or he would find his way in another aspect of the music business. Andre kept him near and continued to collaborate with him on songwriting. Eventually, the D.O.C. lost his home, and Andre allowed him to come live with him and Michel'le.

N.W.A. had brought on a positive change in Andre's finances. From my point of view, and judging from his accomplishments, I thought he was doing exceptionally well. Problems started to arise within the group, which brought on major disagreements. The group that started out as Dr. Dre, Easy E, D. J. Yella, and Ren had made changes and now included Dr. Dre, Easy E, Ren, and Ice Cube. The confusion among the group, and their management caused the group to break up. Ice Cube was the last to come and the first to go. Eventually, Andre left, and N.W.A. was no more. By now, I knew that Andre was very smart and could recognize when he was not being fairly dealt with. I think that this, among other disagreements, caused him to take a long look at his position. Andre recognized his talents. He had grown confident in his decision making, and, most important, he knew his worth.

News of the group's demise became known, and there was rivalry between Easy E and Andre. Each of them began dissing one another through their messages in their songs.

I soon received the news that Andre had joined up with another record company—Death Row Records. This group was under the management of a man named Suge Knight. I immediately saw Andre become better off financially, and with that came happiness. Suddenly, there were a number of engagements to attend. There were performances, parties with many celebrities in attendance, and an abundance of award shows. There was a part of me that was very happy for the financial success that Andre had attained, yet there was another part that yearned for the old way of life that we once had. Perhaps I would be much happier if I could have the best of two worlds—Andre's presence and his financial success. Maybe this sounds selfish, but I would take the family togetherness over money any day. He became very busy, and the only way we would get to see him was by going to his house or visiting him at the studio.

I was stunned by the news when Shameka told me that she was feeling kind of weird, and the diagnosis turned out that she was pregnant. We started planning right away for her prenatal care to ensure that we would have a healthy baby. This would be my seventh grandchild. At that time Tyree had one son, Shameka had one on the way, and Andre had one son and four daughters, to my knowledge. When Shameka found out she would be having a little boy, I started working on decorating Shameka's room for the baby. We moved Shameka downstairs to the guest bedroom. The months went by so fast, and Shameka grew bigger and bigger.

Approximately one month before the baby was born we gave her a baby shower. There were about 175 people that participated. Andre rented a mansion in Calabasas and hired caterers, bartenders, and decorators. Everything was perfect. All of the people showed their love by showering her with gifts—so many, in fact, that she did not have to purchase anything for her baby. It was a wonderful thing that Andre did for his sister. When the shower ended, Andre told us to come to his house to spend the night with him, so that we would not have to drive all the way back to Placentia that night.

The next day we were all gathered in the kitchen for breakfast when Andre walked in and said, "You're all are invited to the celebrity basketball game," where he was to make a presentation. We excitedly jumped up from the table and dispersed to go get ready. This was our first time attending the celebrity basketball game, and we all enjoyed it tremendously.

One day, I was sitting at home creating some African fashion ideas when Andre called. He said he was calling to let me know that he was sending me a surprise. I was so overjoyed that I could not think about creating designs anymore. When the doorbell finally rang, a smiling gentleman stood on the steps. He identified himself and told me he was there to deliver my surprise. He asked me to step outside, handed me some keys, and pointed to a brand-new white Mercedes. I screamed, ran to it, jumped for joy, and cried tears of joy. When I finally came back down to earth, the gentleman went over all the functions of the car with me. I don't think I heard too much of what he said. I was still shaking with excitement. I knew I must have been a special mom. I felt like the luckiest person in the world. After the gentleman left, I couldn't wait to get back inside to call Andre, and thank him for such a wonderful gift. It was hard to find the right words to express what I felt.

By this time, I had grown tired of the little money that I was making working through the employment agency and decided it was time to come up with an alternate plan. I remembered that the African accessories I made and displayed in my boutique had sold like hotcakes during Black History Month. I had to come up with a gimmick to get people to be proud to wear fashions made from African fabrics all the time, and not just to look upon them as costumes. I came up with the idea of designing suits and sportswear with African flare made from beautiful African fabrics. The thought struck me when Warren wore an African crown to work and people started asking where he purchased it. He told me about the conversation, and asked if I could make the crown. I told him I could. Warren said, "If you make them, I will sell them." I immediately drafted a pattern, and the next day I went to downtown Los Angeles to purchase fabrics. As fast as I could make the crowns, Warren would sell them. A few weeks later Warren came home and told me that a co-worker asked if I could make an entire African outfit. I had never attempted to make an African outfit, but felt secure in telling Warren to tell his coworker that I could. "Never say can't" was another one of Mom's words of wisdom, and it has followed me nearly all my life.

That night I drafted a basic pant and dashiki pattern to add with the crown. I took care in purchasing the "just right" prints from the many wonderful choices. Needless to say, the outfit that I created was designed with quality as well as style. Warren delivered the outfit the next day. He returned home with money, a story of how his co-worker expressed his satisfaction, and orders for three more outfits. Suddenly, I had a full-time job at home. When I wasn't filling orders, I spent time designing and creating patterns for dresses, suits, swing coats, and pant sets with matching crowns for ladies, and suits and jackets with matching crowns for men. I developed an interesting mix of men's and women's fashions, sent out invitations to friends and relatives, and held a fashion show in my den with seventy-five guests in attendance. The guests were amazed at my fashion ideas, and I received so many orders I found it hard to keep up. My workday started getting longer and longer. I received requests to do fashion shows for others, including one in Chattanooga, Tennessee, and another in Atlanta, Georgia. This trend went on for months. Even though I had created a steady flow of cash, prior to that I had gotten way behind in the bills, and was struggling to play catch-up.

Andre came to the rescue on a couple of occasions, but as fast as I caught up on one bill, another was due. Soon I started to see other designers developing African fashion lines, and I also saw many African boutiques popping up. I saw more and more people wearing the fashions, which was good, but it also meant competition for me. I knew it was time to move on to another unique idea, before I ended up feeling down-and-out again.

I felt good when LaVetta (one of the mothers of Andre's children) told me, "Verna, you were the innovator of this phase of African styling." She went on to say, "You are before your time with fashion ideas."

During a gathering at Andre's house, someone in my family sidled up to me and sniffed that she never would have thought that Andre would become a rapper "because he always seemed kind of square." Offended and surprised, I replied, "Just because he wasn't gangbanging or trying to act hard and stupid did not mean that he was square. I taught him that he could be bad with his mind. While you were gangbanging, he was focusing on what he wanted to do with his life. Look what it got him." I stalked away, thinking that it took a lot of nerve to sit in a man's backyard and bad-mouth him at the same time.

Later down the road, Andre ended up helping this family member out of a financial jam. Once again I thought about what she had said, and I smiled.

SiXTEEN

Andre Takes a Wife

ONE DAY ANDRE called and asked that Shameka and I meet him for lunch. He said that he had something important to talk about. We met with Andre at Monty's on Wilshire Boulevard. Little did we know that Andre had invited us to lunch to announce that he was getting married. At first Shameka and I laughed hysterically, and finally we figured out that he was drop-dead serious. You see, we didn't think that Andre would ever get married. We had heard that announcement a few times before. I was very surprised, but happy for him. Shameka and I were both anxious to know his bride-to-be. When he told us that his choice was a young lady named Nicole, I was even more surprised, because as far as I knew, he had not known her very long.

The news of Andre's plan to marry Nicole spread like wildfire. By the time we got home, our phone was ringing off the hook. Most of the calls were from people expressing congratulations, surprise, or confusion. Then there were also those, mainly females, expressing their dismay. I felt that Andre had made his decision, and whomever he chose to marry, if she made him happy, I was happy for him.

After planning for a big wedding to include all their friends and family members, the couple settled on getting married in Maui, Hawaii, with only a selected few present. It was a warm tropical wedding on May 25, 1996. I had a nice break away from the problems I left at home, but reality soon settled in upon my arrival back home. I picked up a handful of bills that I had no earthly idea how to pay. I asked Andre for help only when things got completely out of control. This was a time to call on him for help again.

Andre invited me to his home for an announcement party. When I arrived, I was surprised to see a chosen few guests casually sitting around. My first thought was, *What kind of a party is this?* My eyes flooded with tears of joy as Andre made the announcement that he was leaving Death Row Records and starting his own record company to be so eloquently named Aftermath Records. Everyone stood up and applauded to show their support for the wonderful news, and then we made a toast to wish him the best of luck. I traced the path from where he had started, the ups and downs, the struggles, the worries about the crazy stuff that was going on with Death Row, and finally to the success of Andre making it to where he worked so hard to get to.

Indeed, this was a time for a celebration. I was partially relieved, but not sure of what I was feeling. I suddenly thought, *Is there going to be a problem for Andre to leave Death Row? Are they just going let him walk away, or are there going to be repercussions?*

Warren and I started arguing more and more about our finances, and finally we decided that a separation would do us both good. Of course, the bills got completely out of control, but I felt that happiness for both of us was more important. Once again Andre came to the rescue. This time he sent me out with a real estate agent to search for a house in the San Fernando Valley so we could be closer. I was excited because I thought I would be close enough for Andre to visit me sometimes, and I was thrilled that he was actually buying me a house. After many days of searching for the perfect house and viewing many, many options, we finally decided on the best house. Once again, I felt like I was that very special mom, and I said to myself, *What a wonderful son I have.*

The thought of leaving our house in Placentia was sad. It was a nice house that was very special to me and held fond memories of holiday gatherings and parties, and it seemed that Tyree's spirit made an occasional visit to check on us. Even though I had mixed emotions about the move, I cherished the fact that Andre wanted to do this wonderful thing for me, and I made myself ready for the move. The day quickly rolled around when we actually moved from Placentia to our new location.

I had not ventured out too far from our new home, so from what I had seen, I didn't think there was much more to the city. It seemed like a small country town surrounded by mountains. Even the shopping center was designed to resemble a quaint little country town. After venturing out, I realized that anything you could possibly think of could be found on Ventura Boulevard. As I got used to the place and ventured farther out, I grew to like it better and better.

When we moved into our new house, the first thing we did after settling in was schedule a house blessing. The pastor, members of our church, and selected friends and family members were invited. The purpose for this ceremony was to rid the house of evil and bring happiness into the home. The ceremony was performed by everyone gathering for prayer in each and every room in the house. Afterward, we gathered in the kitchen to continue the celebration by rejoicing over food and beverages. After adjusting to our new home, and familiarizing myself with the area, I went out on a job search. After going on many interviews and being turned down for various reasons, including my credit rating, I was just about ready to give up.

Can you imagine not hiring a person because of a blemished credit report? Usually, bills get behind because of a change in income, so how can you pay the bills without a job? Bad credit does not mean that a person is a bad person. It does not mean that they are not trustworthy. Everyone has been late paying a bill for one reason or another, and they definitely don't make bills with thoughts that they won't be able to pay them. Things can happen to cause a drastic change in income such as illness, layoff, or even death. Sometimes I think that the laws are designed for the working people, the so-called middle class. The rich don't have a problem, the poor are being taking care of by the working-class taxes, and the "middle class" suffers through all the laws and weird rules.

I went to a nearby fabric store to purchase fabric to make two of my grandchildren Halloween costumes. I noticed the sign in the window: "Now Hiring." At the time, I was only interested in purchasing the fabric. As the days went by the thought of sitting around doing nothing got the best of me, and I had the urge to go on a job hunt again. Remembering the sign at the fabric store, and knowing I could be an asset to the store, I went there to apply. I was hired, almost immediately, and worked my shift and sometimes was called in on my off days. I enjoyed working there because being around fabric delighted me more than a little kid in a candy factory.

During the time that I was working, Andre started giving me a weekly allowance. Once again, I was overjoyed with his generosity. When Andre found out that I was working he tried to talk me out of it. He would say, "Why are you working? Why don't you quit that job?" Each time I would come up with an excuse. I told him that I would quit as soon as I got enough money to buy new tires for my car. The next thing I knew he was sending me out to buy a new car. This time I got a brand-new Jaguar. I didn't stop working at that time because the store needed me.

One day I was sitting back and thinking about setting goals, and what I really wanted to do with my life. I knew that fashion was my first love, so I put all concentration in that direction. Sometimes I would sit and take a walk down memory lane. These were the times when I would think about where I've been, and where I could go without making some of the same mistakes, or at least how to do something that I had my heart set on more. You know, "if at first you don't succeed, try, try again." I thought about the business venture with Nadine, and the fact that if I had known how to make patterns then, I would not have been in the partnership with her, and I would not have been disappointed in my decision to work with her. I feel that for every negative thing that happens, a positive can come from it. Nadine had a great influence over my decision to learn pattern making.

With that thought, I started doing a little research on design schools. I came across a school called the Fashion Institute of Design and Merchandising (FIDM). I knew that I could pass the fashion course with flying colors, create my own fashion line, and feel my independence again. Upon visiting FIDM, I decided that this was definitely what I wanted to do, so I signed up to take the entry exam. I told Andre about my decision to go to school, and he thought it was a wonderful idea. Andre was the only man left in the family. He had also established himself as our main support and comfort zone. It also felt good to do something to make him proud. I thought that the best way to repay Andre for his many gifts, and acts of kindness, was to make him proud of me.

After passing the entry exam at FIDM, I called Andre to tell him the good news. He and Nicole congratulated me by sending me a beautiful bouquet of flowers. That made me feel wonderful, and it gave me the incentive to go for it full force.

The first few weeks at school were exciting. There was a lot taught that I already knew, but there was so much that I didn't know. The homework was overwhelming. It was almost as if I was married to FIDM. There was no time for anything else but schoolwork. I was determined to learn as much as I could. I was trying hard to continue working while going to school, even though the schoolwork took up a lot of my time. I would hear some of my classmates discussing their full-time job, school, and homework, and told myself if they can do it, certainly I can. All of them were young, and some of them straight out of high school. I had to face the fact that I was triple their age, and my energy level was not quite like it used to be.

One day I was at work, helping a customer with a fabric selection. When she made her decision, I found an empty spot at the cutting table and proceeded to the fabric. One of the managers came over to the table and asked me if there was a reason I decided to take her spot at the cutting table. I told her that I did not know it was her spot; I was only interested in helping the customer. She went on to say that she had just stepped away from the table for a minute, and I had taken her spot. The customer felt bad and apologized for the problem. I told her she didn't need to apologize, finished assisting her, and sent her on her way. That just happened to be a day when I was scheduled to be off, but another manager asked me if I would come in to replace a sick employee. I finished the shift, but as soon as I arrived home, I called in and quit. I told the manager who hired me what happened and that I didn't appreciate the manager talking crazy to me in front of customers when I was only doing my job. She told me that she had had a few problems with her, too, and that she would be going to another location soon. My decision to quit was a weight lifted off me that allowed me more time to spend on my schoolwork and also satisfied Andre's wishes.

I met many interesting people at FIDM with each session. The work got more interesting and more difficult. The classes went so fast I thought there was no way that anyone could retain it all. It always seemed to me that the curriculum was set up to push you straight on through in a short length of time. There were people attending FIDM who didn't speak very good English or know very much about sewing. I often wondered if they understood everything that was being taught, and if they would have a problem keeping up. Even though I had been sewing for years, and some of what was being taught I already knew, I found it difficult at times to keep up myself. One morning I completed homework from three classes in time to take a shower, dress, and go to class. I had stayed up all night long, only to get to school and receive the same amount of homework. After beating myself up trying to keep up, retain what I had learned, and find time to go over what I had done wrong, I started to get discouraged. The corrections that I needed to go over were few, but I just needed the time to absorb what I had learned. I had almost convinced myself that I would have perhaps done better if I were younger, with a higher energy level. I didn't want to fail at something that I wanted so bad.

The final decision was to take a time-out from school to go over what I had learned up to that point, so that I could be sure that I would retain what I had learned. During my last days at FIDM, I met a gentleman named Bernard who was employed as a security officer at the front desk near the elevator to the parking structure. He would sometimes help me carry my bags or the large rolls of muslin or pattern paper to my car. One day we exchanged phone numbers, and we began to have interesting conversations about social issues. I was always surprised to find that he shared some of the same opinions about social issues that I had. I was even more surprised to find out that he lived only five blocks from my mother's house in the neighborhood where I grew up.

It was near Christmas, and my cousin Lois invited me to her job's annual Christmas party. During a conversation with Bernard, I mentioned the party, and he told me that he would like to go to the party with me. I was excited and called Lois to tell her to reserve two tickets for me and my guest. Prior to the date of the party, Bernard and I discussed who was picking up whom. I decided that I would pick him up since the party was near his house, and there was also the fact that I wanted to be in control of the first date. I gave considerable thought about allowing a man to be a gentleman, which involves picking a lady up, but I didn't want him to see where I lived. After that date, aside from seeing Bernard at school, we started spending time together.

Bernard would always encourage me to reach my goals. I believed that if I set my goals high, if I only made it halfway, I would have reached a great accomplishment. He had this crazy belief that I had an unbelievable amount of rare talent. For me, that was like a dose of medicine that kept me pumped up and feeling energized. I really had my hopes set on designing and marketing a fashion line. At least that way I would be able to exercise what I had spent time and money learning at FIDM.

I spent a lot of time studying what I had learned and practicing the pattern-making phase of the studies. I started sketching ideas of hip-hop designs and found that I really had a hard time with that. I would sometimes sit with pad and pencil in hand without a clue as to what I wanted to do except the basics. I was never satisfied with any of it because it didn't grab me as being anything unique. I knew that the younger set were the biggest consumers of fashions. This was my reason for trying to design a hip-hop fashion line.

One day I was talking to one of my nephews, Tony, a.k.a. Jinx. When he asked what had I been doing, I told him about how I had been trying to design a hip-hop fashion line. Upon telling him the problems that I was having coming up with ideas, he told me that hip-hop was out of my league. He said when he thought of me, he thought of unique, sophisticated fashion. He thought that this had a great deal to do with the problems I was having coming up with design ideas. I gave what Tony said a lot of thought. That evening I tried sketching fashions that I would wear, and it was unbelievable how the ideas kept popping into my mind. The thought came to me, *Out of the mouths of babes come words of wisdom.*

One day I came up with the idea to do a his-and-hers loungewear line. I sketched the ideas, and went out researching the fabrics. I chose the name Dre V Denee for the label. I thought it had a nice ring for a loungewear line. The name was derived from parts of my name and my children's names. "Dre" was for Andre, "V" was for the first letter of my name, and "Denee" is Shameka's middle name. I brought my idea to Andre's attention, and he committed to putting up the start-up money. I never wanted to sit back, doing nothing, while Andre or anyone took care of me. My son had put me in a fabulous home, bought me a wonderful car, and set me up to receive a weekly allowance. I thought that the best way to repay him for his kindness was to do something profitable for myself. It felt good for my son to think enough of his mom to share his wealth, but I also wanted to be independent. After all, heaven forbid, what if something happened to the music business—what would we do? I thought it would be wise to have something to fall back on.

I had samples made from the designs I chose for the Dre V Denee loungewear collection. I decided to put on a fashion show as a survey to see how people accepted the loungewear. My guest list included special family and friends. After giving a lot of thought to the type of fashion line I wanted to create, I realized there were many reasons for settling on loungewear.

I thought about how people dating will always show their best. They show their best attitude, their best hairdos, their best charm, and especially their best dress, completing an all-over great personality. I noticed that after the first romance was over, couples start deviating from the well-groomed look and revert to looking plain or sometimes shabby. The idea for the line was to create a look for at-home wear that could be worn to lounge around the house, to entertain in, and to look good for one another. My slogan was "Sexy appealing but not so revealing."

The show was a success, and the response was helpful in giving me the courage to try out my idea. I pulled off the show with four models: two ladies and two gentlemen who strutted their stuff on a runway that led from the french doors of my living room out to the middle of my backyard. With 125 guests dining, socializing, supporting my ideas, and truly enjoying the fashions displayed in the show, I was confident that my idea was a winner. Even though Andre was working that day and could not be there, I felt that he was there in spirit, supporting his mother's efforts.

Andre made life very easy for me. I didn't have to want for much. Andre set it up where I didn't even have to see a bill, and I am very thankful for all that he has done for me. I look back on where my son came from and all the trials and tribulations that he has endured. Stardom is really a hard status to claim. It affords you everything that you could possibly want, but it comes with a lot of struggles. I guess anything worth having you have to work hard to keep. Along with success comes a whole lot of "just-now friends" and "just-now relatives." This leaves you to wonder which of these people are hanging around to show love for Andre or Dr. Dre. I always wanted to be there for Andre as he was always there for me. I never wanted to see him hurt in any kind of way. People that didn't seem kosher to me, I would watch. I would sometimes issue little warnings to Andre to be wary of some of these people, but I didn't want him to think that I didn't think he could take care of himself. A caring mother doesn't care how old her children get; there will always be room for worrying about their well-being.

I would get want-to-be artists trying to come through me to get to Andre. Different ones would call me with sad stories of needing money for a variety of problems. I would always wonder why they thought I had money because my son had money. The list of requests for money was for homes on the verge of foreclosure, the need of new cars, and hospital bills, and some were bold enough to ask for money with no obvious reasons. I have always been a giver, so my heart would go out to some of them, especially the ones who had children and were losing their homes. Soon it got a little overwhelming, and I had to start saying no. The funny thing about all of this is when I fell a little short, I could never get anything from any one of them. How quickly people forget kindness, or was it just a "sucker play"?

Another problem I had was visiting friends and relatives and being introduced as Dr. Dre's mom. It was like I no longer had a name. I never let on to people that I was Andre's mom for fear of people treating me differently, and I tried to be careful of my surroundings. There were times when I had parties, and Andre would be bombarded by people who had known him all of his life, but yet he would spend most of his time signing autographs and taking pictures with them. There were also people who would wait for the opportunity to catch him off by himself to ask him for money. Andre started asking me who was going to be at my parties to determine whether he and Nicole wanted to attend. When he did accept an invitation to a party, I started monitoring the people approaching him, so I could shortstop the action. I would tell them that there would be no autographs or picture taking this night, because he came to enjoy, not to work.

SEVENTEEN

Shameka

SHAMEKA AND I would bump heads sometimes and get into some heated arguments. I seem to think that it is very hard for two women to live under the same roof. At times, I would think my daughter had moved out of her body, and a demon had moved in. I wanted to say, "Who are you? And what have you done with my daughter?" I learned to walk away, and give her an opportunity to go somewhere and think about it, for fear that I might half kill her if I got ahold of her. There was a time when she pushed me beyond my limit, and when I came to myself, I found myself on the floor, on top of her, with my hands around her throat while she was struggling to say, "Somebody help me, because she's going to kill me!"

After that, if she entered into a debate that may have had the possibility of evolving into an argument, she would do it with caution. I could not see going through the pains of bringing somebody into this world, and doing without sometimes so that they can have, and then turn around and have them talk to me crazy. I thought, *Oh, no, something's truly wrong with this here picture.*

Well, it took me a while to get over the shock of seeing what was once an obedient little girl turn into what I thought was a rebellious little wench. As I went along wondering why my daughter was suddenly challenging me, I one day got my answer from watching a talk show. As I sat down to eat lunch one day, I turned on the TV, and a talk show just happened to be on. The topic for the day was mothers who have problems with their daughters. I noticed that the daughters ranged from the ages of twelve to nineteen. I was appalled by the way these girls talked to their mothers. It was at that time that I realized that some girls go through a phase in life when they struggle for womanhood. At least this was my own opinion of the situation. After all, my sons never gave me any lip, so it had to be a female thing. Although my daughter and I had our run-ins, at times she was just like my best friend. We did a lot together. As a matter of fact, at times I would tell her, "Don't you want to do something by yourself sometimes?" Most of the people that were in my circle, meaning the people that I allow to be close to me, envied me for the relationship that I had with my children.

I had everything that I could possibly want, thanks to Andre, of course. I was so used to being independent that it was hard for me to remain idle for any length of time. I would also encourage my daughter to strive for better. We would frequently encourage one another, always trying to figure out ways to make money for ourselves.

Andre also reached out to his sister, Shameka, by giving her a weekly allowance. I always believed that if you become too content with what you have and stop reaching for better, then the world will soon catch up and pass you by. Back in the '90s I remember telling a friend that my million-dollar house would someday be considered a mediocre house. The friend responded by saying, "It will be a long time before this house will fit that description."

Within a few years, I saw houses that made mine look like a maid's quarters. Andre actually lives in a house that is a good example of that. I could walk upstairs, go in a room, come out, and get lost in his house. The outside perimeter of the grounds that surround his beautiful home are huge also. It's unbelievable how fast things progress. Before you can get a brand-new item, a new and improved one is already in the making that makes the one you just purchased obsolete.

Shameka and I put our heads together at times to figure out ways to start our own businesses to make money. Of course, we would make these plans, hoping to have Andre to help us get the initial start. We would usually run our ideas past Andre for approval when we could take him from his busy schedule long enough. If he thought it was a good idea, he would give us the initial help.

Shameka came up with an idea to do a children's clothing catalog. She worked very hard at putting together a perfect business plan and presented it to Andre, and he actually liked the idea. After giving it some thought, he decided it wasn't something that he wanted to fund. He may have found something in the plan that he didn't think would work out. Needless to say, Shameka was disappointed because she had invested a lot of time, research, and a few dollars of her own money on something she was so sure of. I encouraged her not to give up the idea and to try to make it work on a smaller scale with her own money.

Even though I appreciated everything that Andre had done for me, and was absolutely proud that he cared enough to want to do nice things for us, I thought we were becoming too comfortable with relying on him for so much. I thought that if we created a way of being self-supporting, we could relieve Andre from some of the support. After all, Andre had many kids that I knew took a big chunk of his money for support. I also thought about what would happen to us all if, heaven forbid, Andre lost all of his income for some reason. I knew if something drastic like that happened, Shameka and I had a solid plan working for us, and we could be his backup plan.

Shameka ended up tabling the idea for the children's clothing catalog until she could manage to save up enough money to fund the idea. In the meantime, she continued to seek better-paying jobs.

Through the years I've encouraged her to go back to college and finish her degree. Andre has also offered her some incentives to encourage her to finish. Because of her love of caring for her child, and buying nice things, I think she chose to work and spend any leisure time taking her child to see various parts of the world. I refer to Shameka as the "sales queen." She is so good at finding unbelievable sales that her friends actually come from miles away just to go shopping with her, and pick up on a deal or two themselves. Shameka is a very giving person and is always involved in helping someone out of a jam, or helping with plans for their special events. I guess she learned some of my habits and took them and ran with them.

Shameka became very interested in real estate, and started educating herself on foreclosures in particular. I noticed that she had a real determination to succeed at doing something successful for herself and her son, Kion, who was approximately two years old at the time. I can remember a time when she worked two jobs and was trying to get a third, part-time job. I convinced her that it was a lot for a lady to work one job and care for a small child, much less three jobs. I told her that her son would eventually wonder who the stranger was in the house whenever he got the opportunity to see her. I did convince her that it was too much, and she began to seek one job that would provide her with the income to live comfortably. I really think that she had become accustomed to getting her own and learned to always reach for more. I would always say, "The Lord gave you five senses. Use them, and there's nothing like earning your own." I would always repeat that old cliché, "A mind is a terrible thing to waste." One thing that I can truly say is, "I didn't raise no lazy children."

Shameka managed to swing a real estate deal and pull a family out of foreclosure by taking over the property and allowing them to pay rent to her and remain in the house. This turned out to be a plus for both her and the family. She went in the deal making money because of the equity that had accumulated on the house. Sometimes I would be extremely surprised at the ideas she would share with me. I would always say, "If there's a way to make money, she will figure it out."

I thought back to when Shameka was a child. She was fortunate to have started preschool at the age of three and kindergarten at four. She was a fast learner, extremely smart, and very eager to learn. The fact that she started school so young meant she would graduate from high school younger than most of her friends.

As a young child, she was very competitive with her brothers. There was an eight-year gap between her and Tyree, and she was often challenged to act above her age. Having two brothers much older was good in a sense, because they would always push her to learn things. I remember when she was four and first learned to ride a bicycle. Andre and Tyree took the training wheels off her bike. One stood at one end of the street where we lived, and the other took a position just far enough to give her enough riding space to be able to catch her if she fell. From my living room window I watched the boys let go, while both of them yelled out instructions to her. She would always strive to show them that she could do what they told her to do. Well, after a couple of trips back and forth between Andre and Tyree, she had mastered riding her bike without the training wheels.

Back when the Atari video game first came out, I was surprised to know that Andre and Tyree were making money with it. They would challenge their friends to play against their little sister, and bet that they couldn't beat her. When the friend accepted the challenge, they would tell her she had better win. Needless to say, she had mastered the game, and her challengers would always leave defeated. Of course, when I found out that Andre and Tyree were taking bets on their sister, I ordered them to stop. Even though I was very stern about them stopping, I thought it was funny, and I gloated over her being so darn smart.

The bad part about having brothers eight and eleven years older was they went places that she couldn't go, and she would be left behind with me. I think that's why she always stuck so close to me. I saw her challenges in almost everything she sought out to do. Aside from being an excellent student all through school, she was good in volleyball in junior high school, and basketball and track in high school.

Shameka didn't give me many problems during her school years. Most of my unscheduled visits to her school were to straighten out unfair situations between Shameka and the teachers. Once when she was in junior high, she called me at work to tell me that one of her teachers pushed her, causing her to fall backward over her backpack. I immediately left work to go to the school. When I arrived, I asked Shameka what she had done for the teacher to become angry enough to push. She said she approached his desk to ask a question, and he pushed her away, telling her to go sit down. The fact that he was a man, pushing a little girl, and could have caused her to injure herself certainly ruffled my feathers. I took Shameka to the office to report the problem. There were also classmates who accompanied us to the office to be witnesses to what had happened between Shameka and the teacher. The office personnel documented my complaint, and we took off to go find the teacher to talk to him about why he pushed my daughter. Everywhere we went, he had just left, so we didn't get to talk to him. Maybe it was best that I didn't find him, because I was very angry and may have reacted in a bad way.

The only other problem was when Shameka was in her last year of high school. She got kicked out of her parenting class for working on homework from another class. This one ended up being the most stupid excuse ever for a problem. I came home from work one evening, and Shameka announced that I needed to make an appointment to see her parenting teacher. She said the teacher kicked her out of the class, and she couldn't return until I had a parent-teacher conference. It was just before spring break, and I had a lot going on. I called to attempt to make an appointment right away, but was unable to reach the teacher to schedule an appointment. After spring break was over, and a few weeks had passed by, I had forgotten about the conference.

Shameka came in one day and asked when I could talk to her teacher, because she had been sitting in the library during the parenting class, and was afraid she would lose the A she had earned in the class. I told her I had forgotten all about it and would call her right away. I made four attempts to meet with the teacher by calling her. I asked if we could meet one day after school, or before school, and even asked her to pick a date and time before giving up and coming to the conclusion that she simply was making excuses not to meet with me. I tried one more unsuccessful phone call to the teacher and finally went to the school to talk to the principal.

When Shameka explained to the principal why she was kicked out of the class, he summoned the teacher to the office. After he reviewed Shameka's past report cards he was convinced that the punishment she received was harsh. All of her grades were good, and all the other teachers' comments stated that she was a pleasure to have in the class. This teacher had actually kicked Shameka out of the class because she had finished the assignment in that class and was completing homework for her math class. When I asked her what should she have done besides just

Verna in Cancun.

Andre and Nicole on
their wedding day.

Roberta (Verna's mother) at
Andre's wedding in Maui.

Shameka in Maui at
Andre's wedding.

Andre in the Carribean.

Nicole and Andre with Tyler (four) and Truice (one), November 1998.

Kion and Cedric with cousins, watching Andre play piano.

Andre's daughter Summer
Young, 2006 (age twelve).

Marcel Young,
age fourteen.

Shameka and Andre.

Trya Nicole Young,
December 2001.

Kaylon, King, and Kion,
Shameka's children.

Truice, Tyler, and Summer,
Andre's children, and Mark
Miller, Shameka's fiance.

Cedric (Tyree's son) on prom night.

Shameka's children, Kion and twins King and Kaylon.

Verna and Shameka.

Aunt Johnnie (Theodore's sister) and Andre.

Verna, Roberta, and Shameka, January 2004.

Verna and Elaine
(Curtis Crayon's sister).

Andre's dad, Theodore, with
Andre and Nicole's son Truice,
at a neighborhood reunion.

sit there, she said she could have been reading a magazine on parenting. I thought that was a stupid response, and apparently the principal did too. He requested that the teacher agree to Shameka stopping by her class to pick up her assignment for the day, and go to the library to complete it. He also gave Shameka a hall pass to come and go without being cited. She had only a few months left before graduation, and he did not want to see her lose an A in the class for absenteeism.

It seemed as though I was constantly running to the schools for one kid or another. I learned that my presence at my children's school was important. They knew that I would come to their school if there was a problem. Even though I would be there to discuss their problems and make sure that they were dealt with fairly, I wouldn't uphold them when they were wrong.

When I decided to go back to school and further my education, it felt good to be able to take advantage of an opportunity that I missed out on when I had Andre. I once read a horoscope that said Aquarius people are creative. Maybe that explains why I was interested in learning everything I could about creating things. Aside from academic subjects, I enrolled in many creative classes, such as stained glass, jewelry making, millinery, shoe covering, floral design, cake decorating, and interior design. I believe everyone should have something to fall back on in case a job doesn't play out. I figured that out of all the creative knowledge that I had soaked up, I never would have to be completely broke. During my life when my financial status was very low, I used these skills of creating things to make extra money. As long as I have a breath of life in my body, I will be determined to make it.

I've always enjoyed entertaining friends and family. My house has been known to be the place where everyone is guaranteed to have a good time. I didn't get out a lot to parties and such, but anytime I felt the need to see my friends and family, I would throw a party. When holidays came near, people would start calling to ask, "What are we doing for Easter, Christmas, New Year's, the Fourth of July, Memorial Day, Thanksgiving, Labor Day, and Super Bowl Sunday?" I would simply say, "Well, I'm cooking," and they'd show up to join in the fun. I would always cook a variety of food, because I knew that food made people happy. There's nothing like having a nice group of fun people together to bring joy to my heart. I have always surrounded myself with children, so people know that children are always welcome at my house.

EIGHTEEN

A Big Mistake

THE MANY YEARS that have passed by have brought me so many wonderful memories. I often look through all of the many pictures of the children, and their children, along with all the parties and other events I've shared with the other special people in my life. It makes me smile to look at pictures and see the stages that these people have gone through, how much some have matured, and remembering the greatness of the ones that are no longer with us.

Being a grandmother is a wonderful thing for me. I see my grandchildren, and I see my children all over again. The genes in our family must be very strong, because each and every grandchild born is marked with my children's looks, and some of them have their personality traits.

Being a free-hearted person sometimes tends to get me into a few situations. I also have a problem with speaking my peace, and saying what's on my mind, which has also presented me with problems. The funny thing is that people know that I will bend over backward to help most of the people in my circle of friends and family. Because of that, some people tend to look at me as if I'm an alien from another planet, because they don't encounter people like me very often. They think I'm a "pushover." I have helped many people out of situations, whether it be money or lending my time to do various types of favors. Most of the time I would do these acts of kindness without a thought of getting paid. I learned a long time ago not to set myself up for disappointment by not making it a habit of asking for help from others. Sometimes I won't even ask Andre for help. I will try to fix the problem myself, and usually I will work it out. There are a few people in my circle who I don't have to ask for help; they will automatically jump right in there and help, then fuss at me for not asking for their help. These special people are my sisters-in-law, Elaine Crayon-Goodman and Johnnie Young-Craig; my girlfriends Cheryl Anderson, Julia McMichael, and Shirley Jackson; and, of course, my children.

Through the years, Warren and I remained friends and would keep in contact. We would have telephone conversations, keeping each other updated on friends and family members who had passed, and what was going on in each other's lives. We were actually better as friends than we were when we were married. Later, I had thoughts that my tax status as well as my assets could stand a chance of being affected by my marital status, so I pursued getting a divorce. I sought legal representation to go through the steps to end the marriage. On October 31, 2002, my divorce became final.

I felt that I wanted to do things to build my financial worth. Even though I never thought that Warren would cause me any problems as far as my assets were concerned, I felt better knowing that whatever I had would go to my children if anything happened to me.

As time went by, I enjoyed being alone and doing as I pleased more and more. I did entertain the idea of having a mate. The question always entered my mind of whether I would meet someone who would hang around me because I was connected to Dr. Dre, or if they really loved me for me. Keeping that in mind, whenever a man drew my interest, I would have a conversation with him, paying close attention to everything he said. Later, I would ease into revealing my high-quality style of living just to see what kind of effect it would have on him. If I discovered a sudden change in his attitude, I would lose interest. I found that men as well as women would sometimes react differently about me when they found out that I had a connection to Dr. Dre. They would either treat me like I was royalty of some sort, or occasionally I would run into someone who was a hater. My children, my mom, and my sister-in-law Elaine were the people who were closest to me, and I spent most of my time with them.

After a few years of being alone, I became closer to my friend who I met at FIDM, Bernard. He and I would talk a lot. He would always talk about how he felt the world should be. Ironically enough, his visions were somewhat the same as mine. This would bring about long and interesting conversations that we both enjoyed having. We started doing a lot of things together, and I also found out that we enjoyed doing a lot of the same things. This included simple things like going to the movies, taking a ride out to the beach, going to a hot-dog stand, and, the most enjoyable part, going to weekend yard sales. We started spending more and more time together, and soon we were together nearly 24/7.

When I introduced Bernard to Shameka, she was overjoyed at the fact that I had a boyfriend. Because Shameka would always include me in plans for trips and various outings, she started including Bernard in all the plans. When Andre met Bernard, I really didn't know whether he liked him or not. Andre has a way of not showing emotions, and he can do a pretty good job of faking. I think Andre started including Bernard in plans to satisfy me. We went to Hawaii, Las Vegas, concerts, and various parties. I've always treated my children's friends as if they were mine, and it was not a mystery as to why they treated Bernard accordingly. We were all like one big happy family.

Bernard was what some would consider a "country boy." He did not live in a big, fine house in an upscale neighborhood. He didn't wear a lot of fancy clothes or act like he was anything more than what he was. I have never been the type of person that would be attracted to someone because of the material things they owned, their status, or their money. Nor was it all about looks, either. I believed that the best beauty in a person comes from within. Throughout my life I learned to love a person from the inside out, and not for their worth or good looks. It never phased me to learn that some people thought Bernard was not my type.

Bernard lived in a small house, with one bedroom and a den, that was within five blocks of my mother's house. His backyard was what I referred to as "Green Acres." He had several breeds of dogs, including a rotweiller, two pit bulls, and a mastiff. He also had a rabbit, a duck that eventually made a nice meal for one of his vicious dogs, and countless pigeons.

I remember talking to Bernard on the phone when we first met. When he told me that he stayed at home a lot and his leisure time was spent in his backyard watching his birds, I imagined he was watching exotic birds. I found it quite hilarious when I found out that he was actually talking about pigeons. I knew then that he was very interesting and unique.

Although Bernard enjoyed attending our functions, he knew that he was not meeting everyone's expectations. That bothered him to the point that he became quiet and a little standoffish when he was around certain people in our circle of friends. There were times when we would get into heated discussion about my friends and how he thought they felt about him. Even though it would make me angry that he was letting me know how he felt about my friends, I was sympathetic, knowing his feelings were being hurt.

Bernard was jealous, which is something that everyone has a little of, some more than others. The fact that most of my friends were guys didn't make it any better. Bernard and I had lots of good times when we were alone together, but I started to see a pattern of problems when we were around friends. I started hearing negative comments through the grapevine more often than usual. I even heard that someone talked about where he lived. When I told my mother what was being said about where he lived, she told me, "It's not where you live, it's how you live." I believe that to be true. A person should not be judged by the area where they live, the clothes they wear, how much money they make, or the type of car they drive.

During the time that Bernard and I were together, he never asked me for anything. He never showed that he was bothered by the fact that I had more money or better things than he had. At one time in his life, Bernard was doing very well financially, according to his own stories and stories I heard from some of his family members. Unfortunately, he had got himself into a financial bind that he obviously was too embarrassed to talk about. He kept his problems to himself, so no one knew the extent of his problems.

One night I fell asleep at Bernard's house while watching a movie, as I had done many times. The next morning I was awakened by the constant ringing of the telephone. Being only half awake, I could hear Bernard constantly describing his house and saying how much it was renting for. First of all, I thought it was strange, because Bernard's phone hardly ever rang. He didn't have very many friends that he associated with. He was what one would describe as a loner. I slid out of bed, showered, and dressed. The phone continued to ring. All day long there were people running in and out of his house as he led them on a tour of it. I finally took the opportunity to ask, "Okay, Bernard, what's going on?" He replied, "I have to rent my house out to keep from losing it." He then explained to me that he had gotten himself in such a financial bind that included having money deducted from the little money he was receiving. I asked him why he didn't ask for help, and he said he did not want to bother me with his problems. That's when I was absolutely sure that Bernard was not hanging around me for my money, which was one of the things I had heard was said about him.

I spent a few days helping Bernard pack and clean his house, as a friend would. I also thought to ask him where would he go from there. I worried that he would not be able to survive anywhere if he could not survive in his home. I really felt sorry for him. He told me that he had plans to start over again once he figured out a way to make some extra income. Bernard was very knowledgeable about real estate, and he had wonderful ideas about how he could make money and afford a good life. I knew Bernard was very comfortable being in his own place, but I offered to let him come and stay at my place for a month or two until he got back on his feet. I knew the gossip would be going full-blast now, but I didn't know any other way to help him. It's funny how most of the people doing the gossiping had more problems than the law would allow. I lived in a gated community, living a pretty clean and wholesome life, and didn't bother anyone. It was hard for me to understand why people spent so much time worrying about what was going on with me.

Bernard and I started having arguments, and that was not good in my house. After all, I was trying to help him, and there was no way I was going to let someone talk crazy to me in my house. Bernard had lots of problems coping with his situation, and it was hard for me to understand what was going on with him. We broke up several times because he was dealing with someone that was just as hotheaded as he was. I refused to bow down and let him take any control of what I did, how I ran my household, or anything else that an adult should be able to do. Each time Bernard threw a tantrum, he would leave but come back quickly with an apology. We went through this drill several times. Some would probably ask why I allowed him to come back. I tried to imagine myself with the many problems he had, and I could understand why he was often on edge. As he approached one problem, three or four more would surface. Aside from me caring a great deal for him, I kept thinking he would figure out sooner or later that I was not the enemy. I thought he would also figure out that I was the one person who was trying to help him.

Eventually, Shameka started to dislike Bernard and would find anything about him to complain about. Usually she would go to Andre with her complaints. I've noticed that when someone does something that's viewed as being wrong, it seems like everything they do becomes wrong. It's the same thing when someone is disliked. No matter what the person does, it's just not good enough. When I shared with Bernard how my children felt about him, he'd say, "I don't know why they don't like me. I've never done anything to them." I would say, "When you do something to their mother, indirectly you've done something to them." The arguments that we had never became physical, but some of the things that were said could cut like a knife.

One day my daughter came to me with a real estate deal. The owner was in default, and was going to lose the property. Shameka's boyfriend's sister was a real estate agent, and she would come across properties in default all the time. Shameka told me I could make money on the property if I could put up the initial money to bring the payments current, and then the owner would sign the property over to me. She also mentioned the fact that the property came with $120,000 worth of equity. I told her that I was saving my money for something else and didn't want to risk not being able to meet my deadline. She asked me if I would loan her boyfriend the money so that he could make the money off the deal. Shameka's boyfriend was a very nice, trustworthy young man, so I told her I would loan him the money. It sounded like too good of a deal to pass up, and I felt that one of us could profit from it. He promised to have my money back in time to meet my deadline. The day that I was to give the loan, Shameka's boyfriend's sister called, asking if I could make the loan in two separate money orders. I agreed to do that, and wrote down the names to whom the money orders were to be made out and the amounts. When I went to the post office to get the money orders, I accidentally switched the amounts. When they realized the error, they called me to ask if I could take the money orders back to get them corrected. Shameka's boyfriend told me that he would take them back to keep me from having to do it, and I agreed.

Bernard overheard this conversation with Shameka's boyfriend and asked me what was going on. I didn't think anything was wrong with telling him the story about the property, and how I was helping by loaning Shameka's boyfriend the money to make the deal. Hearing how much money Shameka's boyfriend stood to make off the deal, he started asking me why I hadn't allowed him to make the money. We were on our way out the door to go take care of some things in Los Angeles. We got into his car, and he continued to ask me why I hadn't considered loaning him the money to make the deal. I asked him if I had, how was he going to pay me back? He went into talking about ways that he could have paid me back that didn't seem reasonable, and definitely did not fit into my time frame of meeting my deadline. I explained to him that I could not take that risk, and that Shameka's boyfriend was sure to get the money back to me before my deadline. After going through a few rounds of why I couldn't loan him the money, and me explaining why, Bernard got frustrated. Seeing that he was not getting anywhere with his proposition, he got angry, and yelled out, "Why don't you go f— Shameka's boyfriend?!" I was shocked at the statement, and while riding along on the freeway, I started throwing everything that was movable at him. Bernard pulled off the freeway, and jumped out of the car. As Bernard walked around on my side of the car, yelling obscenities, I jumped out, ready to defend myself. He approached me as if he was going to hit me, and I readied myself to go to war. When he realized what was about to take place, he told me that he didn't want to fight me, because he knew that he would have to deal with my son. I was so angry until I told him, "My son is not here right now. You're dealing with me, and when I finish with you, then you might have to deal with my son." At that point we returned to his car, and I told him to take me home. Instead, he drove me all the way to Compton, making several stops to take care of his business. I was so upset at what Bernard had said to me that I cried all the way to Compton and all the way back home. Not only was what Bernard said to me degrading in the sense that he suggested that I should do something awful with my daughter's boyfriend, but it was also not acceptable for him to have a problem with what I did with my money.

After returning home, I went to my bathroom to take a nice, relaxing bath to help relieve the tension. The more I thought about what he had said, the angrier I got. To top it off, he kept coming in the bathroom to apologize. Instead of apologizing and leaving it alone, he continued to justify why he felt that way. All that did was make matters worse. When I finished my bath and dressed, he came back to reason with me, furthering the conversation as to why he felt that I should have helped him be opposed to helping my daughter's boyfriend. We ended up in a yelling match, and I told him to just go away and leave me alone. He continued talking, and I blew up. I had two walk-in closets in my bathroom. One closet is where I kept my gun, and there was another closet directly across from that one. I stormed out of the bathroom, went to the closet, and got my gun. At that time, Bernard ran into the other closet, and locked himself in. He continued talking madness, and I fired a shot into the closet on the end where I knew he couldn't possibly go. It was meant for a warning, and I did get him to stop talking. As the echo from the shot cleared, I didn't hear any more. He was so quiet, I did worry that I had hit him. I grabbed my keys, went outside, got in his truck, and drove to the park that was just outside the back gate to our community. On the way I saw my daughter, her boyfriend, and my grandson jogging. I waved to them and proceeded to go to the park. I went there to calm down and to think about what I should do about this situation. A few minutes passed when I looked up and saw my daughter's boyfriend pulling up beside the truck. He told me that Bernard had called the police, and for me to take his car and let him drive Bernard's truck back. I didn't want him to be involved in such a mess, so I told him to go back. While he was talking to me, my daughter called him on his cell phone to tell him that not only were the police at my house, but they were also accompanied by the SWAT team. After telling him to go back, I drove off and got on the freeway, not knowing where I was going, or what I actually was going to do.

After passing three exits the thought came to me that I was on the freeway and my family was back at the house, possibly being harassed by the police. I got off the freeway, and headed back home. On the way, I stopped at a gas station near the house to get a cup of coffee to help calm my nerves. As I was walking out, my daughter and grandson drove up to the gas station, pulling up beside my car. Her boyfriend drove in from another entrance. Shameka ordered me to get in her car and told her boyfriend to get my purse containing the gun out of Bernard's truck and to meet us back at the house.

Shameka dropped me and my grandson at home and went back to the gas station. By the time she got back to the gas station, the police were there, questioning her boyfriend. The police took Bernard's truck and my purse to the police station. When Shameka returned home, she told me she had contacted Andre's attorney, alerted a bail bondsman of the possibility of my arrest, and alerted relatives. Andre was out of the country on a well-deserved vacation at the time. I was hoping that he did not get the news there and ruin his vacation.

Later that night the attorney called to inform me that he had spoken to the police and asked them to let me get a good night's sleep; they would arrest me in the morning. Early the next morning my phone started ringing off the hook. People from every-where had heard the news, and were calling to see if I was all right. Most of them knew that these actions were out of character, so they were very concerned that I had been beaten and provoked into shooting at someone. The attorney came to my house to ad-vise me, and he told me that the police would be coming to arrest me. He said, "As soon as they arrest you, the bail bondsman will be there to meet the bail." He also told me that I should be very proud of my daughter, because she did everything right as far as contacting the right people. I was arrested, went to court, and re-ceived punishment for my actions. That was an experience that taught me to calm my temper, and it also taught me not to ignore the signs of abuse, whether they are verbal or physical. Some-times words can hurt worse than a lick.

Bernard called several times asking for my forgiveness for his actions. I was so angry at the time that I didn't want to talk to him much less think about accepting an apology. He even showed up at one of my court dates to tell the judge that he didn't believe I had intended to hurt him. This made the D.A. very angry, because they really wanted to give me whatever the maximum punishment was. There were many wonderful letters sent to the judge from friends and family stating the kind of person they think I am.

These things were part of the deciding factor that kept my pun-ishment at a minimum. When Andre came back, he said he was greeted at the airport by some of his friends telling him, "Man! Mom is in trouble!" When he called me I was so apologetic, because I knew that this was bad publicity for him. What a mess I had made, and I was so very sorry for it. All of this happened because I was trying to help someone, and this didn't seem like a just reward for being good to a person. I had thought about changing my ways, and becoming a mean and selfish person, but that was not in my nature at all, and I found it very hard to go through the motions.

This became another lesson in life that taught me about self-control. After anger management classes, and a lot of soul searching, I restored my self-worth. I have two wonderful children, fifteen grandchildren, five great-grands, and a mother, all who depend on me to be there for them, not to mention a number of friends.

I would say to anyone who is faced with a situation where they are backed into a corner to think rationally before you come out swinging. You may do something that can change your life and the lives of others drastically. Through this lesson, I vowed to never let anyone push my buttons again. I learned to be in complete control of myself. It's like my mom always says, "Every tub has got to sit on its own bottom."

NINETEEN

The Road Ahead

SHAMEKA AND HER son Kion's dad had many, many problems. When they broke up, I thought it was for the best, because they seemed to be unhappy most of the time. She had one boyfriend that was the sweetest person you would ever want to know, but Shameka seemed to be very distant from him. As a matter of fact, I found myself telling her on a couple of occasions, "If you don't like him, let him go. Don't just keep him around and hurt him." They ended up breaking up as well. When she started dating a male stripper, I thought, "Oh, my God, where is this going?" He was a very nice person from my perspective, but he kept me worrying about my daughter. He was constantly studying up on making fast money, and in the interest of it all, it cost him his life. That was very sad. Here was a young man in the prime of his life, with the most pleasing personality, who had taken the wrong path in life, and perhaps he got so deeply involved that he couldn't turn around.

Then she met Mark, who became the love of her life. Shameka had a certain glow when she was around Mark, and when she spoke of him. I knew he was the one she would cling to, because I didn't see her react that way with the few others. She had a different type of pep in her step when they went out together. And when they would walk, she made sure she walked with him instead of way ahead of him, as I often saw her do with her ex-boyfriend. Mark treated Shameka special, and would always show the little twinkle in his eye that made me feel like he was truly in love with my daughter.

One day Shameka called to tell me that she felt a little ill. I advised her to go to the doctor. After a few days of continuing to feel ill, she finally took my advice and went to the doctor. Boy, was I shocked to hear that I was going to be a grandma again! After all, at that time, Kion was eight years old. The second shock was when she was approximately seven months into her pregnancy. They performed an ultrasound, and found that she was having twins. How excited I was, but she didn't seem happy at all. She was caught up in thinking about all the negatives of having two kids at one time. I convinced her that it would be all right. She had Kion and two grandmothers to be her and Mark's helpers.

On January 19, 2005, Shameka gave birth to two healthy little boys. Because they were born on Martin Luther King's birthday, and also because Andre had suggested the name, she named the first-born King, and the other Kaylon. On the night that the babies were born, I spent the night at a friend's house and was fast asleep when they tried to call to let me know that Shameka was being rushed to the hospital. When I got home the next morning, the phone range just as I walked in the house. It was Mark, calling to tell me that the babies had been born. I was excited to hear that I had two new grandbabies, both weighing in well over five pounds. I was disappointed that I missed the blessed event, but was happy to hear that Andre and Nicole were there.

Mark and Shameka had purchased a fixer-upper house in a nearby city. They worked on it diligently all the way up until the babies were born. Upon calling a company to install forced air to the house, they found out that there was asbestos in the house. Andre panicked when he heard about it. He told them to move back with me, and he would help them buy a better home. Andre did follow through with the purchase of a beautiful home for Shameka and her family. Once again, I was overjoyed as I thought about how wonderful it was to see how my family looked out for one another. Andre didn't have to share with us, but we knew that his gifts of love were straight from the heart.

In March 2006, Mark proposed to Shameka, and she said, "YES!" I asked Shameka what type of wedding plans they had discussed. She told me that they wanted the type of wedding that their families and close friends could attend. Shameka and I excitedly started jotting down ideas and following through with the plans.

I made her dress, the bridesmaids' dresses, the junior bride's dress, and outfits for the host and hostess. Through all the running around, designing, sewing, and normal daily chores, I also managed to make my dress and take care of many of the details to make her wedding a most memorable occasion. There were times when I would stress out, but I had fun assisting in putting a wedding together for once in my life.

The wedding date, May 19, 2007, came around rapidly. Aside from a few problems that occurred before the ceremony, the wedding was the most beautiful wedding that most had ever seen. With its tropical theme, there were many tropical colors and flowers that set the mood, along with a steel-drum player, dancers in native costumes doing their traditional island dance, and a fire dancer. This was the setting for a wedding with a host of wonderful friends and family. There were thirteen bridesmaids and a maid of honor, thirteen groomsmen and a best man, a junior bride and groom, a flower girl, two ring bearers, an usher, and a broom bearer. The wedding began with my cousin Darryl Evans chanting the spoken word while the groom strolled down the aisle to the altar. My cousin the Reverend Ron Evans officiated. The crowd wept with tears of happiness as they were surprised by Shameka's son Kion, aged eleven, who sang her entry song, "I'm Marrying an Angel," by Jamie Foxx. I was filled with tears of joy as Kion sang and I watched Andre usher his little sister, Shameka, down the aisle. Now I have a new son-in-law and members of his family to add to my circle, and I love them.

The guests consisted of many family members and friends, some of whom came from far-off places. One friend, Honnie Seng, came from Australia but was not able to attend the wedding because three days prior to the event she had to be rushed to the hospital for emergency surgery. I visited her after the wedding and kept in touch until she was able to return home.

How lucky can a mother be? Aside from having more than I ever wished for, thanks to Andre, I am rich with the most important thing to me—a wonderful family. With Tyree missing from the chain, and my dad gone too, I find myself clinging to my son, my daughter, my mother, and any of my grandchildren that will allow me to stay close to them. I know that they are more important to me than any amount of wealth or materialistic things. I want to spend any available time with them. I just can't imagine my life without my children. Now that they're grown up and have found their perfect mates, I know sooner or later there will be a separation between mom and children. I had never been alone before in my whole life, so the thought of not having any of my kids around was hard to visualize. Many times throughout their lives I would make statements about looking forward to and being glad when they were grown up and out on their own. I think that I did a lot of bluffing back then. Even though I could imagine the peace and quiet, I remember the old cliché, "Be careful what you wish for." I knew that I would be just fine for a minute, but it wouldn't take long for me to miss them.

Now that the last child has left my house to live on her own, I have a lot of quiet time to think about what I would like to do at this stage of my life. I thought about forming a group that would be geared toward helping women and teen girls with their self-esteem, etiquette, and fashion choices. I would also like to dibble and dabble in the event-coordinating profession. I am currently taking classes in floral design, which is something that seems to take me out of this world and into a special place for a moment in time. That place is a place of beauty and fragrance that allows me to create unique designs without limitations. I also take cake decorating, which has proven to be a skill that I could definitely make a living with if I needed to. I have made several cakes of various designs for many occasions. People seem to enjoy the taste of my cakes, and they tend to be fascinated by the various shapes, themes, and decorations I design. I may consider taking a few courses in culinary arts to enhance my love for preparing meals for large gatherings. All of these are skills that would go hand in hand if I decided to pursue the challenges of being an event coordinator. I also still enjoy my special love of creating fashions.

I plan to keep busy as usual, but not busy to the point that I cannot continue to be a loving mother, daughter, grandmother, great-grandmother, and friend.

$$\begin{array}{r} {}^{3\ 4} \\ 10.68 \\ 5 \\ \hline 5340 \end{array}$$

$$\begin{array}{r} 534 \\ {}^4 3\!\!\!2 \\ \hline 58.74 \end{array}$$

$$\begin{array}{r} {}^3\ 1\ 2\ 5 \\ 2\,9370 \\ 4 \\ \hline 1\!\!\!,17480 \end{array}$$